Latin
American
Government
Leaders

Latin American Government Leaders

SECOND EDITION

Edited by

David William Foster

Published by the
Center for
Latin American Studies
Arizona State University
Tempe, Arizona
1975

Library of Congress Cataloging in Publication Data
Main entry under title:

Latin American government leaders.

    1. Statesmen—Latin America. 2. Latin America—
Biography. I. Foster, David William. II. Arizona
State University, Tempe. Center for Latin American
Studies.

F1407.L37 1975   920'.08   75-15809
ISBN 0-87918-021-8

Published in the United States of America

Printed by Affiliated Lithographers

Typeset by Text Craft, Inc.

Bookbinding: Hard Covers by Roswell Bookbinding
                 Soft Covers by Neal Bindery, Inc.

Bureau of Publications 45207

Preface

The first edition of *Latin American Government Leaders* was published by this Center in mid-1970. Within a very short time, because it filled a major gap in reference materials, all copies had been sold. Within a longer, but no less brief, space of time, the entries in that 1970 edition were, in many important cases, obsolete. Latin America during the late sixties and the early seventies has seen a large number of governmental changes: witness changes in the latter part of 1973 in three important areas like Chile, Argentina, Uruguay, virtually the whole "Cono del Sur." Therefore, both the reception of the first compilation and the need for an updated listing have motivated this new edition.

Most of the sections have had to be prepared from scratch, while a few simply required updating rather than fundamental changes. We are grateful for the time and effort of compilers who have worked with us on this revised edition, and are pleased with the contributions of established scholars as well as of promising graduate students. It should be noted that the several sections, because of the different individuals involved, will manifest necessary variations in style. Special note should be taken of the assistance lent by Lewis A. Tambs, Director of the Center, for his many recommendations concerning aspects of this project.

Countries are, as opposed to the geographical arrangement of the first edition, presented in alphabetical order.

David William Foster
Professor of Spanish
Chairman, Editorial Board

Contents

Argentina

Compiled by
Lyman G. Chaffee
Associate Professor of
Political Science
California State College,
Dominguez Hills

Alende, Oscar.

Candidate of Alianza Popular Revolucionaria — a left center coalition supported by the Partido Comunista in the March 1973 presidential elections. The coalition made up of the Partido Revolucionario Cristiano, Partido Intransigente and Unión del Pueblo Argentino. Polled 8% of the national vote, obtained 12 seats in the Chamber of Deputies. Alende refused to be a candidate against Perón in the presidential elections of September 1973. Alende was a member of the UCRI Party. Broke with the party over differences with Frondizi in 1963. Candidate for president in 1963 on the UCRI ticket, obtained 16.8% of the vote. Ex-governor of the province of Buenos Aires.

Alfonsín, Raúl.

Leader of the left wing faction within the Unión Cívica Radical. Opposes the controlling Balbín faction. Opposed the Balbín participation in election negotiation with Perón on the possibility of an election alliance. Alfonsín faction, supported by the youth groups, called the Movimiento de Renovación y Cambio (MRC).

Alsogaray, Álvaro.

Organizer and leader of the party Nueva Fuerza, which obtained 2% of the presidential vote in the March 1973 elections. Conservative group with strong financial support in the business and professional class. Represents the essence of liberalism. Influential politician since 1955. Ex-presidential candidate for the Partido Cívico Independiente which he founded, ex-ambassador to the United States during the Onganía government and early supporter of the military coup of 1966, cabinet member in succeeding governments since 1955, and candidate for federal deputy in 1963 and 1965 on the party Reconstrucción Nacional; lost both times.

Anaya, Leandro Enrique

Appointed Commander of the Army by President Perón in November 1973, replacing General Jorge Raúl Cárcagno. General Anaya's father, Laureano Orencio Anaya, was a Peronista, army general and friend of Perón during his first presidency. Was originally recommended by a group of Peronista officers to President Cámpora as Commander of the Army but passed over. Selected by Perón because he didn't have the prestige and leadership quality of Cárcagno, who constituted a potential military threat with his personal qualities as a possible future caudillo. Anaya was a personal friend of ex-Commander of the Army and ex-president of Argentina Lanusse who in 1971 appointed him head of the Tenth Brigade, situated in Palermo. Promoted to rank of General.

Antonio, Jorge.

Influential Peronista political figure of the first Peronista era. Industrialist. Exiled in Uruguay. Owner of the influential weekly *Primera Plana*.

Arnedo Álvarez, Jerónimo.

Secretary-General of the Communist party of Argentina. Important figure in swinging the Communist party to supporting the election of Perón in September 1973. The party was precluded from offering its own candidate as the electoral law still prohibited it from participating in the elections under that label. Justified this position because of the surrounding of Argentina by military dictatorships which did not want to see a populist Argentine progressive government. Hopes the Communist party of 50,000 will win full legal rights. Arnedo is one of the co-founders of the party along with Rodolfo Ghioldi, both in their late seventies. Rejuvenation drive to increase membership to 200,000 and bring younger communists into leadership position of the central committee.

Balbín, Ricardo.

Lawyer, old time leader of the Unión Cívica Radical. President of the National Committee of the UCR. Twice second in the two presidential elections of 1973, obtaining 24% of the votes against Perón in September 1973. Prior to election, speculation was he and Perón would work out a unity presidential ticket with Balbín as vice-presidential candidate. Support within UCR rests with the majority of party caudillos and caudillejos. Considered by the UCR youth as a regressive bureaucrat. Presidential candidate against Perón in 1951, again candidate against Frondizi in 1958.

Barcena, Bernabé.

Important labor leader of the 62 Organizaciones de Córdoba. Elected one of its two secretary-generals. Represents the orthodox line aligned to the bureaucrats of Rucci. Conflict with the *legalista* faction headed by Atilio López.

Bidegain, Oscar.

Elected Peronista governor of the important province of Buenos Aires, 1973. A representative of the political sector of the Movimiento Justicialista. Strong ties with leftist Peronista youth and leftist forces within the movement. At odds with the vice-governor, a labor sector representative. Criticized strongly by Perón and under political pressure from labor bureaucrats.

Calabró, Víctor.

Elected vice-governor of the province of Buenos Aires. Labor Leader and Peronista. Held the office of Treasurer of National Secretariat of the Unión Obrera Metalúrgica (UOM). Moderate-conservative orientation within the Peronista movement. Linked to López Rega. Nomination due to the backing of the 62 Organizaciones. Represents the labor sector of the Movimiento Justicialista.

Cámpora, Héctor.

Dentist. Elected president of Argentina as a Peronista, March 1973. Took office May 25th, 1973. Close confidant of Perón. Strength rests with the left-wing Peronistas. His candidacy was opposed by the labor bureaucrats at the nominating convention of the Partido Justicialista, December 1972. As president, immediately established the Peronista independent nationalistic foreign policy line by establishing diplomatic relations with Cuba, North Korea, East Germany, Albania, etc. Nonalignment. Resigned the presidency July 13th, 1973 after seven weeks to allow Perón's election. Currently Argentina's Ambassador to Mexico. May be appointed as Perón's ambassador-at-large for Latin America to coordinate the activities of Argentina throughout the hemisphere.

Cárcagno, Jorge Raúl.

Born October 28, 1922. Began his military career March 1939. Designated Interventor of Córdoba 1969 after the "Córdobazo." Accused by independent left of being the suppressor of the "Córdobazo" as he commanded the troops. 1971 Lanusse designated him interventor of YPF. Chief of V Cuerpo de Ejército under whose jurisdiction the Rawson prison falls. Came into national prominence by being appointed Commander of the Army by President Cámpora in May 1973. Represents possible Peruanista line of military nationalist as contrasted to the liberal military faction. Said to have aligned himself closely with the left-wing Peronistas and Peronista youth. Forced to resign by Perón, December 18, 1973 in a move by Perón to consolidate his power within the armed services. Said Cárcagno was being removed because of his leadership ability within the army and his potential as a future caudillo. Charismatic qualities. Backed by the army as man to restore the army's political position and prestige. Known for his anti-North American, pro-nationalist line. Advocated removal of the French and U.S. Military Aid Missions throughout Latin America. Propagated for progressive position within the military. Removed as part of Perón's strategy not to attack the army, but to guard against caudillos. The CGT leadership opposed Cárcagno and his ties with Peronista youth. His resignation isolated the military faction with the closest ties with the Peronista youth.

Cesio, Juan Jaime.

Political aide to ex-Commander of the Army, General Cárcagno.

Architect of the Commander's agreement with the Peronista Youth which led to Operativo Dorrego. Labor bureaucrats in CGT opposed Colonel Cesio increasing influential position, Cárcagno proposed his promotion to rank of General, supported by the Defense Department, but denied by the Peronista Senate majority, along with three other colonels to be promoted to rank of General. This rebuke by the Senate led to General Cárcagno's resignation and the temporary isolation of the Cárcagno faction. Represents a possible peruanista nationalistic line within the military.

Coral, Juan Carlos.

Leader of the executive committee of the Partido Socialista de los Trabajadores (PST). PST groups Marxist, Leninist and Trotskyist revolutionaries. 39 years of age, presidential candidate in the March and September elections of 1973. Polled less than 1% of the vote. ERP guerrilla underground developed under the PST.

Coria, Rogelio.

Important labor leader and past Secretary-General of the 62 Organizaciones.

Dalla Tea, Carlos Alberto.

Considered a progressive within military ranks. Maintained his position as head of the Jefatura de Inteligencia del Estado Mayor General.

Díaz Bialet, Alejandro.

Provisional president of the Senate at the time of the resignation of President Cámpora. Peronista. Next in line for succession for the presidency after the vice president. Politically maneuvered, he was on a European trip at the time of Cámpora's resignation and Congress then elected the president of the Chamber of Deputies, Raúl Lastiri, as interim president, representing the José López Rega faction. This turned the interim government over to the right wing Peronistas.

Diéguez, Rubén Manuel.

Provincial deputy to Buenos Aires province representing Frejuli. From La Plata, Regional Secretary-General of CGT. Member of the Unión Obrera Metalúrgica. Bitterly opposed by left-wing youth as a representative of labor bureaucrats.

Ezcurra, Guillermo.

Important political-military figure. Chief of Operations of the First Army during the Lanusse government. Confidant of Sánchez de Bustamante. Received rank of General with Lanusse's backing. Under the Peronista government, given important position of Chief of the Tenth Brigade, headquartered in Palermo.

Fatigatti, Ernesto Genaro.

President of YPF; retired army colonel. Peronista interventor in the state of Santiago del Estero.

Firmenich, Mario Eduardo.

Ex-fugitive from justice during the Onganía government due to the Aramburu case. Emerged as the leading spokesman for the Montoneros and Fuerzas Armadas Revolucionarias (FAR). Opponent of the CGT labor bureaucrats.

Gelbard, José Ber.

Minister of Treasury and Finance. First appointed to this position by President Héctor Cámpora, May 25th, 1973. This appointment was taken as a step toward the policy of national conciliation and was welcomed by the business community but bitterly opposed by the left-wing Peronista organizations because of Gelbard's close ties with international business. He was past president of the national business organization, the Confederación General Económica (CGE). Director of a major industrial corporation. The CGE has closer ties with the Peronista movement than the more powerful UIA, an anti-Peronista group. Gelbard began his economic activities in Catamarca; one of the founders of the CGE during Perón's first presidency which was an alternative to the conservative UIA. Director of the CGE for many years. One of the three most influential cabinet ministers. Responsible for the Pacto Social with CGT.

Gómez Morales, Alfred.

Appointed by Héctor Cámpora as president of the Banco Central. Previously held the portfolios of Minister of Finance and of Economic Affairs 1949-54, during Juan Perón's first presidency.

Grabois, Roberto.

Leader of Trasvasamiento grouping within the Juventud Peronista. Represents the center position. The Brigadas come under this grouping.

Grondona, Mariano.

Lawyer. Important political commentator in Buenos Aires. Writes column for *Primera Plana*. Was professor of politics at the Escuela Superior de Guerra and the Instituto de Ciencias Políticas de la Universidad Católica Argentina.

Gullo, Juan Carlos.

Leader of the Tendencia grouping of the Juventud Peronista (JP), Tendencia, the most radicalized and powerful of the JP Groups, the Tendencia Revolucionaria, Tendencia Socialista. Good ties with groups outside JP. Tendencia controls three political magazines.

Iñíguez, Miguel Ángel.

Appointed Chief-of-Police, November 1973.

Iscaro, Rubén.

Leading spokesman for the Partido Comunista. Member of the executive committee. PC supported the Alianza Popular Revolucionaria coalition in the March 1973 presidential elections and Frejuli or Peronista coalition in September elections. Supports Perón's united front against the imperialist forces of capitalism. Party ineligible to run candidates as the party lacks *personería política.*

Jaime, Armando.

Labor leader from the province of Salta. Represents the peasant movement of Salta. Leader of CGT rebelde of Salta. Clasista and Peronista. Mentioned as a possible vice-presidential candidate with Tosco for the presidential elections of September on the PST ticket. Adherent of the Peronismo de Base line, which began in Córdoba in the CGT under the leadership of Raimundo Ongaro.

Kennedy, Norma.

Leading woman politician. Member of the feminista branch of the Peronista Movement. Member of Consejo Nacional del Partido Justicialista. Elected to Congress. Served as principal organizer of the National Commission for the Permanent Return of General Perón which organized the June 20th, 1973 welcome demonstration of Perón's return to Argentina. Strong ties with the CGT. Ex-member of the Communist party. Nominated Isabel Perón for vice-president. Involved in several publications, *El 17, La Intransigente.* Fervent and influential Peronista.

Lanusse, Alejandro Agustín.

Ex-Commander of the Army under the Onganía government. Third military president of the 1966 coup. Instrumental in the removal of Onganía and the second military president, General Levingston. Assumed presidency in March 1971. Attempted to reinstate a nationalistic orientation headed by the army. Failed and decided to allow national elections with Peronista participation.

Lastiri, Raúl Alberto.

President of the Chamber of Deputies and interim president after the resignation of President Cámpora. Responsible for setting up and calling of new election for September 23rd, 1973 which led to the election of Perón. Important connections with Perón. Son-in-law of José López Rega, Minister of Social Welfare who was Perón's ex-private secretary while in Madrid. Became interim president because the president of the Senate, Díaz Bialet, was out of the country.

Levingston, Roberto Marcelo.

Military attache to U.S.A. Replaced Onganía as president on June 23, 1970. After nine months in office, removed on March 23, 1971.

Lima, Vicente Solano.

Vice President under Dr. Héctor Cámpora. Appointed by Perón as Secretary-General to the presidency with the responsibility for coordinating the military, political, trade union and youth affairs of the country. This position is in essence a de facto prime minister who will oversee the day-to-day administrative duties. His appointment is seen as a conciliatory gesture to the left-wing of the Peronista party. He is not a member of the Peronista party. Belonged to the old conservative party. Was a candidate for president in the elections of 1952 (Lima-Reynaldo Pastor). After 1955 supported the integration and participation of the Peronista masses. 1963 presidential candidate of the Frente Nacional y Popular that finally was not allowed to compete, having been declared illegal by the military establishment because of the Frente's Peronista sympathies. Gained the confidence of Juan Perón and became the vice-presidential candidate for Frejuli with Cámpora in the spring 1973 elections. One of the two most influential men around Perón. Has the task of holding the Peronista coalitions together.

Llambí, Benito.

Minister of Interior, retired diplomat, conservative. Given the responsibility of trying to put an end to internal terrorism and kidnappings. December 21, 1973 a new agency was established, a Security Council headed by Llambí to enforce the new security law which increased the power of the police as well as the penalties against the illegal use of firearms and subversive acts. This act is directed against the illegal Ejército Revolucionario del Pueblo (ERP). He replaced left-wing Dr. Esteban Righi, Minister of Interior in the Cámpora government who resigned his post with Cámpora.

López, Atilio.

Important Peronista labor leader of Córdoba. Vice-governor of Córdoba Province. Elected one of the two secretary-generals of the 62 Organizaciones de Córdoba. Represents the *legalista* faction or the more leftist combative labor grouping. Opponent of the Rucci CGT faction. The CGT of Córdoba is more militant and rebellious than other groupings within the CGT National Confederation.

López Rega, José.

Minister of Social Welfare. Very close confidant, friend and associate of President Perón. Long time private secretary to Perón. Considered to represent the right-wing tendencies within the Perón cabinet. Has come under tremendous pressure and criticism from the Peronista youth movement. Took a one-month's leave of absence during the last month of Perón's presidential campaign as a conciliatory gesture toward the Peronista youth. Peronista youth, in particular the Motoneros and the Revolutionary Armed Forces (FAR) opposed López Rega.

Manrique, Francisco.

Retired naval officer. Ex-aide to Rojas and Aramburu. Twice candidate for president in 1973 on the Alianza Popular Federalista (APF) ticket. This coalition supported by el Vanguardia Federal and la Confederación Popular Renovadora. Represented the conservative right position. Ran third behind Perón and Balbín in September 1973. Received about 12% of the vote, about the same percentage as against Cámpora. Ex-minister of Social Welfare in the military governments of Levingston and Lanusse. Resigned August 9, 1972 to run for president. Opposed by the military government as a candidate. Election strategy to unite the provincial political discontent of the interior.

Martiarena, José Humberto.

Influential Peronista Senator. Represents the political branch of the Peronista party on the Executive Committee of said group. Party bureaucrat.

Martínez, Ezequiel.

Secretary of Planning in the Lanusse government. Resigned his post to become the presidential candidate for Alianza Republicana Federal and in essence became the Lanusse's government official candidate. The Alianza Republicana Federal was made up of ten provincial parties, conservative in orientation. Leopoldo Bravo, vice-presidential candidate. This Alianza obtained 2.53% of the national vote. Elected 4 senators and 10 deputies. Did not contest the September elections against Perón.

Martínez de Perón, María Estela.

Vice-president and third wife of President Juan Perón. Opposed for this position by the left-wing elements, which considered her conservative. Said to have been selected by Perón in order to avoid or postpone the decision on his succession upon retirement or death and thus avoid a clash between the left and right elements within the Peronista party. Born February 4, 1931 in La Rioja. Met Perón in Panamá where she was with an Argentine Folklore Dance Company. Became his secretary, married Perón in Madrid 1961. Not considered politically astute. Assumed presidency upon Perón's death, July 1, 1974.

Martínez Raymonda, Rafael.

Vice-presidential candidate on the ticket with Francisco Manrique of the Alianza Popular Federalista. Influential spokesman for this party and responsible for its organization.

Miguel, Lorenzo

46 years old. The most influential labor leader. Secretary General of 62 Organizaciones. Leader of the Confederación General de Trabajo. Actual Secretary-General of the powerful and influential Unión Obrera Metalúrgica. Influential Peronista. Member of the Mesa Directiva del Consejo Superior Justicialista. Considered a labor bureaucrat. Politically one of the most powerful individuals in Argentina.

Moreno, Nahuel.

Veteran Trotskyist leader.

Numa Laplane, Alberto.

Candidate for Commander of the Army after General Cárcagno's resignation. Backing from Perón's close friend, Minister of Social Welfare José López Rega. Not selected as Commander, but given important post of Commander of the First Army situated in Palermo. Could well play an important role in future political maneuvers. Jefe de Operaciones del Estado Mayor General during the Cámpora government.

Ongaro, Raymundo.

Union leader of the CGT rebel group, the CGT de los Argentinos, formed in March 1968. CGT de los Argentinos represented forty-three labor organizations with 800,000 affiliated members. Headquarters in the printers union. CGT de los Argentinos represented Peronista Cristiana. No longer influential, as the Marxist groups have abandoned this grouping. Many of the militant trade union leaders developed out of this faction.

Otero, Ricardo.

Minister of Labor. Considered by the left to represent the labor bureaucracy. Labor leader with ideological tendencies, aligned with the Unión Obrera Metalúrgica. Instrumental in working out the Acta del Compromiso Nacional between the CGE and CGT. Nominated by Cámpora from the powerful Unión Obrera Metalúrgica. Ex-Secretary-General of UOM of the federal capital. Imprisoned in September 1955 for a year after the military coup. 1956 joined the UOM and from then rose within its ranks.

Pérez, Félix.

Secretary-General of the important Luz y Fuerza Union (FATLYF, La Federacion de Trabajadores de Luz y Fuerza).

Perón, Juan Domingo.

President of Argentina, 1946-1955. Overthrown by a military coup, September 1955. Army general who rose within the ranks. Became Secretary of Labor, vice-president, Secretary of Defense and president. Married Eva Perón. As head of the Movimiento Justicialista he selected Cámpora as the candidate for March 1973 elections. Elected president in September 1973 after 18 years of exile; died on July 1, 1974.

Puig, Juan.

Minister of Foreign Affairs in the cabinet of ex-president Cámpora. One of Cámpora's two principal cabinet ministers. Noted for his left-wing sympathies and responsible for implementing the beginning of the non-aligned foreign policy of the Peronista government, which saw the quick establishment of diplomatic relations with Cuba and other Communist countries. Forced out when ex-president Cámpora resigned in July 1973. Replaced by the conservative retired diplomat Dr. Alberto Vignes.

Puiggrós, Rodolfo.
Important political author. Author of numerous books and articles. One-time Communist. Became an admirer of Juan Perón, yet keeping his left-wing position. Supporter of the Cámpora presidency in the March elections. Became the Rector of the University of Buenos Aires. Forced to resign this post by the Perón government in October 1973 in the aftermath of the crackdown on certain left-wing groups after the September assassination of José Rucci, Secretary-General of CGT. Popular with the militant university students who opposed his ouster.

Righi, Esteban.
Minister of Interior during the presidency of Héctor Cámpora. One of Cámpora's two principal cabinet ministers and known to have left-wing sympathies. Regarded to be responsible for the general amnesty of political prisoners which took place with Cámpora's inauguration in May 1973. Forced to resign when Cámpora stepped down and the government swung to the right.

Romero, Adelina.
New Secretary General of Confederación General de Trabajo, replaced the assassinated CGT Secretary-General, José Rucci. Front man for Lorenzo Miguel, the power behind the organization.

Romero, Julio.
Two time president of the Justicialista party in Congress. Represents the moderate wing of the Peronista party. Governor of the Province of Corrientes. Represents the political branch of Peronismo.

Rotta, Silvana.
One of the four members of the executive committee of the Movimiento Nacional Justicialista. Represents the Feminista branch.

Rúa, Fernando de la.
Senator from the Federal District. Member of the Unión Cívica Radical. Scored a surprising victory over the Peronista candidate. At 33 considered to have a bright future. Selected by Ricardo Balbín as the vice-presidential candidate against Perón in the September 1973 presidential elections.

Rucci, José.
Dominant labor leader until his assassination September 23, 1973. Killed by machine gun fire as he left his residence. Secretary-General of the Confederación General de Trabajo. Elected to that post in July 1970 and opposed the Ongaro rebel, CGT de los Argentinos. 47 at time of

death. Militant anti-Marxist, a Rosista and Peronista. Member of the Unión Obrera Metalúrgica. Dominated the 62 Organizaciones. Close personal friend and supporter of Perón. Frequent visitor of Perón's in Madrid. Important strategist in Perón's return. Allegedly assassinated by ERP because he represented trade-union bureaucracy but subsequently denied by ERP. Event led to declaring ERP subversive and illegal. The assassination led to a series of political murders, with victims belonging to the left and right-wing Peronista factions.

Salamanca, René.
Leader of the combative Córdoba faction within the labor movement. Leader of SMATA Union. Marxist, Clasista. Opponent of Perón's National Unification. Represents the combative faction within the 62 Organizaciones de Córdoba known as Independientes, no Alineados y Autónomos.

Santucho, Roberto.
Maximum leader of the anti-Peronista guerrilla movement Ejército Revolucionario del Pueblo (ERP). ERP founded in 1970 as the revolutionary arm of the Partido Revolucionario de los Trabajadores. Wife killed in the prison massacre at Trelew, August 1972, in which sixteen guerrilla leaders were shot down in their cells at the naval prison.

Selser, Jorge.
Important leader of the Socialista party. Headed the Socialist faction, Movimiento Socialista para la Liberación Nacional that participated in the election alliance with the Peronistas, Frejuli.

Sueldo, Horacio.
Lawyer. Christian Democrat from Córdoba. Supported the National Reconstruction position. Vice-presidential candidate and leader of the Alianza Popular Revolucionaria. Along with Alende, declined to be candidate in the September elections.

Timerman, Jacobo.
Important newspaper businessman in Argentina. Created *Primera Plana, Confirmado* and founded in 1971 *La Opinión,* an independent daily of moderate-left orientation.

Tolosa, Eustaquio C.
Long time militant labor leader of the Sindicatos Unidos Portuarios Argentinos (SUPA).

Tosco, Agustín.
Leader of the Córdoba ideological Clasista left-wing labor faction along with René Salamanca. Leftist following called Movimiento Sindical Combativo, a faction within the 62 Organizaciones de Córdoba. Opponent of the Pacto Social between the CGE and the CGT. Leader of the

Luz y Fuerza Union of Córdoba. Imprisoned by the military government. Ties with the Communist party. Drafted by the Partido Socialista de los Trabajadores as presidential candidate for September 1973 elections. Declined.

Troccoli, Antonio.
President of the Unión Cívica Radical bloc of the Chamber of Deputies. Longtime influential UCR party bureaucrat. Supporter of Balbín. Previously served in congress.

Vignes, Alberto.
Minister of Foreign Affairs. Retired diplomat. Considered conservative. Appointed by Sr. Raúl Lastiri, interim president. Retained by President Perón. Not thought to be a very influential person within the cabinet.

Yessi, Julio
Aide to López Rega. Peronista youth of conservative tendencies. Appointed to executive committee of the Partido Justicialista as the representative of the youth branch. Member of the Consejo Superior de la Rama Juvenil.

Bolivia

Compiled by
Joseph Holtey
Graduate Assistant in History
Arizona State University

NOTE: Since Bolivian cabinet officials more often hold office for months rather than years, little reference has been made to participants at this level of the nation's politics.

Abecia Baldivieso, Valentín.
Lawyer, historian and professor of philosophy. Born in Sucre, October 9, 1925. Subsecretary of Ministries of Housing and Public Works and Communications. Minister-counsellor to Paris, 1952-1956. Author: *Histografía boliviana.*

Alexander, María Teresa.
Publisher of *Hoy* and *Última Hora.* Bolivian representative to the OAS, January to April, 1970. Bolivian ambassador to U.N., 1969 to April 1970. The first and only woman ambassador to the OAS. Father, Alfredo Alexander Jordán, a publisher, killed by bomb, March 1970.

Arzabe Fuetelsaz, Walter.
Minister of Public Health, 1969. Born in Cochabamba in March 1931. M.D. from University of San Simón. Studied in Barcelona, Chicago,

Venezuela. Written books on medicine. Member of Honra de la Sociedad Brasilera de Oftalmología.

Ayoroa Ayoroa, Juan.

Minister of Government, Justice, Immigration, 1969. Born in Cochabamba on April 11, 1924. Studied at San Calixto and La Salle. Entered Colegio Militar in 1940 and graduated in 1944. Cavalry officer. Professional studies at Escuela de Motomecanización and Escuela de Aerofotogrametría de Brasil, Escuela de Armas Bolivia, Escuela de Estado Mayor y Comando. Commander of the Regimiento Ingavi. Lt. Colonel, career officer.

Bailey Gutiérrez, Alberto.

Minister of Culture, Information, Tourism, 1969. Born in La Paz on December 17, 1929. Father, U.S. citizen from Minneapolis, Minnesota. Studied in Argentina, Barcelona, Córdoba, London, and Columbia University in United States. Co-director and columnist of newspaper *Presencia* in La Paz. Sub-director of cultural journal *Signo*.

Banzer Suárez, Hugo.

President of Bolivia, August 22, 1971-. Born in Santa Cruz, July 10, 1926. Educated in La Paz at Colegio Militar del Ejército. Graduated, 1940. Additional training at School of the Americas, Panama Canal Zone (1955) and Fort Hood, Texas, at Armored Cavalry School (1960). During the 1960s commanded Bolivian Fourth Cavalry Regiment. Minister of Education in Barrientos' cabinet until 1967, when sent to Washington D.C. as military attaché. Director of Colegio Militar del Ejército (1969-1970). Speaks fluent English. Married to Yolanda Parra.

Baptista Gumucio, Mariano.

Professor and writer. Minister of Education, 1969. Born in Cochabamba, December 11, 1934. Graduated from Colegio Bolívar in La Paz. Studied English and English Literature at the City of London College. Executive Secretary of the Bolivian University Confederation. Formally an influential member of the MNR party. Law studies in Sucre and La Paz. Married to Carmen Alvarez. Author: *Revolución y universidad en Bolivia* and *La guerra final*.

Bilbao Rioja, Bernardino.

Career officer, General. Presidential candidate, 1966, on Christian Democratic Community (CDC) ticket.

Bonifaz Gutiérrez, Oscar.

Minister of Mines and President of Comibol, May 1970. Secretary General of the President 1969-1970. Born in Potosí on June 2, 1929. Studied law at Universidad Tomás. Masters in comparative law, Southern

Methodist University. Assistant secretary of mines and petroleum. Married to Susana Paz H.

Céspedes Augusto.

Lawyer, journalist, politician and noted historian and novelist. Born in Cochabamba, February 6, 1904. Director of the newspapers *La Calle* (1936-1944) and *La Nación* (1961-1963). Served in the House of Representatives, 1938-1940 and 1958. One of the founders of the National Revolutionary Party (MNR). Former ambassador to Paraguay (1945-1946) and Italy (1953-1957). Member of the President Villaroel ministry. Lives in La Paz. Author: *El dictador suicida, El presidente colgado,* and *Sangre de mestizos.*

Fortún Suárez, Guillermo.

Former Minister of Information and Labor. President of the Banco del Estado, 1974.

Franco Guachalla, Alfredo.

Lawyer, author and politician. Born in La Paz, September 10, 1925. Minister of Labor since the 1960s. Author: *En torno a la cuestión social.*

García, Ambrocio.

Minister of transportation, 1974.

Guevara Arze, Walter.

Political leader. Born in Cochabamba, March 11, 1912. Separated from the MNR party in 1960 and in 1961 founded the Authentic Revolutionary Party (PRA) and has been its leader since that time. Ambassador to the UN, May 1969. Law degree, Universidad de San Andrés, 1932. Director of Mining Bank, 1939. Professor of sociology at San Andrés, 1940. Secretary-General of the government, 1944. Representative (deputy) late 1930s. Foreign Minister, 1952-1956, 1960, 1967-1968. Ambassador to France, 1956-1958. Minister of Interior, 1958-1959. PRA presidential candidate, 1960. Exiled to Chile, March 1961. Returned to Bolivia but exiled to Paraguay in May 1974.

Gutiérrez, J. Oswaldo.

Influential and very close to administration, probably important figure in Ovando's administration. Minister of Agriculture. Senator from Santa Cruz.

Gutiérrez Gutiérrez, Mario.

Lawyer, writer and politician. Minister of Government 1971-early 1974. Living in Santa Cruz. Leader of Falange (FSB) party since 1959.

Guzmán Soriano, Alberto.

Military man (General). Minister of Foreign Relations, 1974.

Humboldt Barrero, Ciro.
Second in command in the MNR party 1972-1974. Claimed leadership of the party at the time of Víctor Paz Estenssoro's exile in January 1974. Exiled in June 1974 following a minor military challenge to Banzer's government.

Hurtado Gómez, Carlos.
President of COMIBOL (Corporación Minera de Bolivia), 1969-1970. Career officer, General.

Kolle Cueto, León.
Minister 'of Peasant Affairs, 1969. Born in Sucre on August 15, 1927. General, career Air Force officer. Chief of military College of Air Force. Commandant of Air Force.

La Fuente Soto, David.
Minister of National Defense, 1969. Born in Cochabamba on October 5, 1919. General, Career army officer. Ex-commander of Estado Mayor. Representative. Professor in War College. Married Luisa Lea Plaza: four children.

Lechín Oquendo, Juan.
Labor leader and politician. Born in Corocoro, Department of La Paz, 1914. Sgt. in Chaco War (1932-1935). Former Executive Secretary of the Bolivian Labor Movement (COB) and Confederation of Mine Workers of Bolivia (FSTMB). Minister of Mines and Petroleum, 1952-1956. Senator, 1956-1960. Vice-President, 1960-1964. Ambassador to Italy, December 1962-November 1963. Ousted from the MNR, January 1964. Founder of Revolutionary Party of the Left (PRIN), March 1954. Presidential candidate of PRIN in 1964. Exiled to Paraguay, May 1965 to May 1967. In Chile until 1973. In exile in Buenos Aires, Argentina 1973-.

Lechín Suárez, Juan.
Military man (Army colonel). President of Bolivian Mining Corporation (COMIBOL) during Presidency of René Barrientos Ortuño, 1965-1969.

Lema Patiño, Raúl.
Minister of Mines, 1974.

Muñoz Reyes, Jorge.
Geologist, educator. Born in La Paz in 1904. Studied in Ayacucho, Tokyo, Oakland, California, U.C. Berkeley (also postgraduate geology), and at the University of La Paz. Law degree. Director general of Mines and Petroleum. Director of the Mining Bank of Bolivia. Professor at U.M.S.A. Rector-dean at the University of La Paz. President of the National Academy of Bolivian Sciences. Author of numerous works dealing with geography, geology and other mineral sciences.

Ortíz Mercado, José.
Minister of Planning, 1969. Born in Santa Cruz on January 5, 1940. Studied political science and public administration at Buenos Aires. Ex-professor of political science in Argentine universities. Ex-head of Santa Cruz chamber of commerce. Ex-representative in Congress.

Ovando Candia, Alfredo.
President of Bolivia, September 26, 1969 to October 1970. Born in Cobija on April 6, 1918. Educated at Colegio Militar del Ejército. Graduated, 1936. Later attended Escuela Superior de Guerra. Reached rank of Lieutenant, 1940. Captain, 1943. Major, 1948. Jailed as falangist, 1952. Chief of Staff, 1957. Army commander, 1960. Armed forces commander, 1961-1969. Active in events of November 2-4, 1964. Reportedly persuaded Paz into exile, 1964. Co-president with Barrientos, May 26, 1965 to January 1966. Married Elsa Elena Osmite Barrón, President of Bolivia's Youth Council.

Paz Estenssoro, Víctor.
Born in Tarija, October 2, 1907. President of Bolivia, April 16, 1952 to August 6, 1956; August 6, 1960-1964; reelected but overthrown in November 1964. Studied economics and law at Universidad Mayor de San Andrés (UMSA) in La Paz. Soldier in Chaco war. Professor of economics at UMSA, 1939-1943. In Finance Ministry, 1932-1933, 1936-1937. President of Mineral Bank of Bolivia, 1939. Minister of Economy for a week in 1941. Head of MNR party since its official founding in June, 1942. Finance Minister for most of Villaroel administration (December 1943-July 1946). In exile 1946-1952 in Argentina. Ambassador to United Kingdom, 1956-1959. Exile in Peru, 1964-1971. In Bolivia, 1971-January 1974. Living in exile in Argentina. Married, four children. Author: *Aspectos de la economía boliviana,* and co-author of *Pensamiento económico latinoamericano.*

Paz Soldán, Jaime.
Minister of Public Works and Communications, 1969. Born in Cochabamba on August 1, 1924. Career military officer, General. Specialist in army engineering (commander of army engineering). Ex Vice-president of Mining Bank of Bolivia. Professor of engineering at UMSA. Director-General of Planning and Engineering of Ministry of National Defense.

Quiroga Mattos, Jaime.
Minister of Finance, 1974.

Quiroga Santa Cruz, Marcelo.
Minister of Petroleum and Energy. May 1970. Minister of Mines and Petroleum, 1969-1970. Born in Cochabamba on March 13, 1931. Studied law, philosophy, and letters at University of Chile. Distinguished writer of fiction and essays. Author: *Los deshabilados.* National representative.

Was elected National Deputy, 1966.

Roca García, José Luis.
 Minister of Agriculture, Husbandry, and Colonization, 1969. Born in Santa Ana del Yacuma on August 25, 1935. B.A. from Santa Cruz, M.A. from SMU in comparative law, Ph.D. in law from San Francisco Xavier de Chuquisaca. Director of Agricultural Bank of Bolivia. Professor in Bogotá and UMSA. Married to Miriam Sánchez.

Rolón Anaya, Mario.
 Minister of Labor and Social Security, 1969-. Born in Cochabamba on January 12, 1928. Studied political sociology at University of Paris and economic sociology at the University of Mexico. Member of A.N.R. (Nationalistic Revolutionary Action). Editor of *El Diario,* 1964. Minister of Labor, 1967. Author: *Política y partidos en Bolivia.*

Ruiz, César.
 Minister of Foreign Relations and Culture, 1969. Born in Trinidad on September 10, 1921. Army General.

Sánchez de Lozada Bustamante, Antonio.
 Minister of Finance and Statistics, 1969. Born in La Paz on June 5, 1932. B.S. from Cornell University, M.S. from Cornell in economics and social anthropology. Has held these posts: Economist in IADB; Vice-president of Mining Corporation of Bolivia; Assistant Director of the Institute of Agrarian Affairs of Oxford University; Economist in the National Commission.

Serrate Ruiz, Mario.
 Minister of Education and Culture, 1974.

Siles Salinas, Luis Adolfo.
 President of Bolivia, April 27, 1969-September 26, 1969. Vice-president, August 6, 1966-April 26, 1969. Asylum in Chile, September 27, 1969 until 1970. Returned to Bolivia. Writes occasional articles for the literature section of *Presencia* newspaper.

Siles Zuazo, Hernán.
 Lawyer and former President. Born in La Paz on March 19, 1914. Decorated during the Chaco War. Law degree from UMSA, 1939. Representative (deputy) in congress, 1940-1946. Exiled with Paz Estenssoro in 1946. Vice-president, 1952-1956. President of Bolivia, 1956-1960. Leader of MNR revolution, April 1952. Expelled from MNR, June 1964. Presidential candidate for the Christian Democrats, 1964. Exile in Paraguay from September to November, 1964. Asylum in Uruguayan embassy, July 1965. Asylum in Santiago, Chile, October 1966-1973. Lives in Argentina.

Suárez Guzmán, Hugo.
Mayor of La Paz, 1969-. Career officer, General. Minister of Defense, 1965.

Torres González, Juan José.
President of Bolivia, October 7, 1970-August 21, 1971. Born in Cochabamba, March 5, 1921. Educated at Bolivian Military College. Captain, 1952 and Colonel, 1954. Ambassador to Uruguay, Minister of Labor, then Chief of Staff of Armed Forces (1967) during Barrientos administration.

Brazil

Compiled by
Rollie E. Poppino
Professor of History
University of California, Davis
(Research Assistant,
Lawrence J. Nielsen)

ARENA is the acronym of the majority political party, Aliança Renovadora Nacional.

Abreu, Hugo de Andrade.
Career army officer. Chief of President's military household, 1974-. Born 27 December 1916. Entered military service 28 March 1934; promoted to rank of colonel, 25 April 1964; subsequently attained rank of general. Attended infantry officer career course in United States and National War College in Brazil. Past commander of paratroop brigade.

Abreu, João Leitão de.
Civilian politician, chief presidential aide, 1969-1974.

Agripino, João.
Civilian politician and a leader of the majority party, ARENA. Governor of Paraíba, 1966-1971.

Albuquerque, Leonel Tavares de Miranda.
Minister of Health in Costa e Silva government, 1967-1969. Born in Paraíba, 29 July 1903. Studied medicine in Salvador, Bahia and Rio de Janeiro. A physician.

Aleixo, Pedro.
Civilian politician. Vice President under Costa e Silva, 1967-1969. Born 1 August 1901 in Mariana, Minas Gerais. LL.B., University of Minas Gerais, 1922. Professor of penal law, University of Minas Gerais, 1929. Participant in 1930 revolution. Founder of newspaper, *Estado de Minas.* Federal deputy, 1934-1937; president, Chamber of Deputies, 1937. Minister of Education in the Castello Branco government, 1964-1967.

Alkmin, José Maria.
Vice President under Castello Branco, 1964-1967. Former federal deputy from Minas Gerais.

Andrade, João Walter de.
Governor of Amazonas, 1971-. Born 24 June 1919. Entered army 12 April 1940. Promoted to lieutenant colonel 25 April 1964.

Andrade Pinto, Alberto de.
President of the Brazilian Coffee Institute.

Andreazza, Mário David.
Minister of Transportation, 1967-1974. Born 20 August 1918 in Caxias do Sul, Rio Grande do Sul. Entered military service 21 May 1930; advanced to rank of colonel 25 August 1965. Attended and taught at various officer training schools, including Army General Staff College. Reportedly masterminded Costa e Silva's successful bid for the presidency, 1966-1967. Served in secretariat of National Security Council and in SNI (Serviço Nacional de Informação).

Areosa, Danilo.
Civilian politician. Former governor of Amazonas.

Baldinelli, Alysson.
Minister of Agriculture, 1974-. Former state Secretary of Agriculture in Minas Gerais.

Barata, Júlio de Carvalho.
Minister of Labor and Social Service in Costa e Silva and Médici governments, 1967-1974. Labor Tribunal Minister, 1964-1967.

Barbosa, Mário Gibson.
Minister of Foreign Affairs in Médici government, 1969-1974. Born in Pernambuco. Studied law at Recife Law School. Entered diplomatic service in 1937 and served at posts in Houston, Washington, New York, Brussels, and Buenos Aires. Achieved ambassadorial rank in 1961. Under Secretary-General of Foreign Relations, 1967. Ambassador to the United States for a brief period in 1969.

Barcelos, Valter Peracchi.
Politician and military man. Colonel. Vice president of majority party, ARENA, in 1973. Director of Banco do Brasil, 1973-. Past governor of Rio Grande do Sul.

Barreto, Humberto Esmeraldo.
Presidential press secretary, 1974-.

Barreto, Paulo.
Governor of Sergipe, 1971-.

Beltrão, Hélio Pena.
Minister of Planning, 1967. Born in Rio de Janeiro, 1916. Director of MESBLA department store chain. Served in Lacerda government in state of Guanabara.

Boghossian, Zaven.
Career naval officer. Director-General of National Department of Ports and Waterways, 1969-1974.

Boni Neto, Francisco de.
Director of Central Bank of Brazil, 1973-.

Borja, Célio.
ARENA leader in Chamber of Deputies. Federal deputy from Guanabara. Former member of Lacerda wing of UDN in Guanabara Legislative Assembly. Member, Commission on the Constitution and Justice in Chamber of Deputies.

Braga, Nei.
Minister of Education, 1974-.

Bulhões, Octávio Gouvea.
A leading Brazilian economist. President of editorial council for *Visão* magazine. Minister of Finance in Castello Branco government, 1964-1967.

Buzaid, Alfredo.
Minister of Justice, 1969-1974. College professor.

Caiado, Leonino Ramos.
Governor of Goiás, 1971-. Member of powerful Caiado family that has contested for control of Goiás with Ludovico family since 1940s. Past president, Superintendency of Public Works of Goiás, and former prefect of Goiania.

Cals, César.
Governor of Ceará, 1971-.

Câmara, (Dom) Helder Pessoa.
Archbishop of Olinda-Recife since 1964. Born in Fortaleza, Ceará in 1909. Ordained a priest in 1931. Active in Brazilian Integralist Action, a neo-fascist party, in the 1930s. Former auxiliary bishop of Rio de Janeiro. One of the leaders of the "progressive" group at Vatican Ecumenical Council, 1964. President of Catholic Action in Brazil. Well-known opponent of military government. Conferred with Pope Paul VI on Brazilian situation in January 1970. Denounced Médici government for alleged use of torture on political prisoners. Winner of Martin Luther King International Peace Prize in 1970. In same year, nominated for Nobel Peace Prize.

Campos, Hélio da Costa.
Governor of Roraima Territory, 1970. Career air force officer. A colonel.

Campos, Roberto de Oliveira.
A leading Brazilian economist and diplomat. Born in 1917 at Cuiabá, Mato Grosso. Graduate studies at George Washington University and Columbia University. Manager-director of Brazilian National Bank for Economic Development, 1952-1953, 1954-1958. President of same bank, 1958-1959. Ambassador-at-Large, to Europe, 1961. Ambassador to the United States, 1961-1964. Minister of Planning in Castello Branco government, 1964-1967.

Candau, Marcolino.
Director-general of World Health Organization, 1953-1973. Born in Lapa, São Paulo. Graduate of Faculdade Fluminense de Medicina in 1933. Worked with Rockefeller Foundation on eradication of *Aegipti gaubia* mosquito, 1939. Past director of Health Center for Niterói. Served in Vargas government to 1945 and later in National Public Health Special Service. Entered United Nations service in 1959.

Carneiro, Nelson.
Civilian politician. Senator of the opposition Brazilian Democratic Movement (MDB). Leader of movement to legalize divorce in Brazil.

Cavalcante, José Costa.
Minister of Interior in Médici government, 1969-1974. Born 6 January 1918 at Fortaleza, Ceará. Entered military service 8 May 1935; promoted to rank of colonel 25 August 1964. Military attaché to United States, 1955-1956. Federal deputy and governor of Pernambuco. Took part in 1964 revolution. Chief of cabinet under Costa e Silva, 1967-1969.

Carvalho e Silva, Jorge.
Ambassador to Italy, 1974.

Chagas Freitas, Antônio.
Governor of Guanabara, 1971-. A leader of the opposition Brazilian Democratic Movement (MDB). Longtime politician and newspaper publisher.

Cleofas, João.
Civilian politician. ARENA senator from Pernambuco. President of Senate, 1970-.

Coelho da Frota, Sylvio Couto.
Became War Minister in May 1974 upon the death of Vicente de Paulo Dale Coutinho. Born on 26 August 1910, he has been a career officer, cavalry branch, on active duty for forty-two years. He is a graduate of the

Brazilian Escola Superior da Guerra, and appears not to have attended any professional schools abroad. He was serving as chief of the Army General Staff at the time of his appointment as Minister of War.

Corsetti, Hygino Caetano.
Minister of Communications, 1969-1974. Career army officer. Born 26 February 1919. Entered military service 1 April 1939. Reached rank of lieutenant colonel in December 1961. Attended Signal Officer career course in United States.

Coutinho, Vicente de Paulo Dale.
Minister of Army in Geisel government, 1974-. Career army officer. Born 5 November 1910. Entered military service 28 March 1928; advanced to rank of general 25 November 1964. Attended Armor Officer career course in United States. Chief of army general staff in Médici government. Died on 24 May 1974.

Couto e Silva, Golbery do.
Chief of Civilian Household of presidency under Geisel, 1974-. Career army officer, a general. Former director of SNI (Serviço Nacional de Informação).

Dantas, Wanderley.
Governor of Acre, 1971-.

Delfim Neto, Antônio.
Minister of Finance in Costa e Silva and Médici governments, 1967-1974. Born 1 May 1928 in São Paulo. Professor of Economics, University of São Paulo. Prolific writer on economics. São Paulo state Secretary of the Treasury, 1966. *Visão* magazine "Man of the Year," 1970.

Dutra, Tarso.
Civilian politician. Federal deputy. Minister of Education, 1967-1969.

Falcão, Armando.
Minister of Justice, 1974-. Ex-federal deputy. Minister of Justice in Juscelino Kubitschek government, 1956-1961.

Faraco, Daniel.
ARENA congressman from Rio Grande do Sul. Elected First Vice President of the Chamber of Deputies, 30 March 1970. Minister of Industry and Commerce in Castello Branco government, 1964-1967.

Fária Lima, Floriano Peixoto.
Career naval officer, vice admiral. President of Petrobrás under Médici, appointed in 1973.

Ferreira de Aquino, Heitor.
Private secretary to President Ernesto Geisel.

Figueiredo, João Baptista de Oliveira.
Head of National Information Service (SNI), 1974-. Chief of Military Household in Médici government. Career army officer. Born 15 January 1918. Entered military service 9 April 1935; advanced to rank of general after 1964 revolution.

Fontes, Geremias de Matos.
Governor of the State of Rio de Janeiro, 1966-1971.

Fontoura, Carlos Alberto da.
Ambassador to Portugal, 1974-. Head of National Information Service (SNI) in Médici government, 1969-1974. Career officer. Born 23 September 1912. Entered army 9 April 1931; advanced to rank of general after 1964 revolution. Attended Army Command and General Staff Officer course in the United States.

Fragelli, José Manoel Fontanillas.
Governor of Mato Grosso, 1971-. Twice federal deputy from Mato Grosso. Past secretary of justice for Mato Grosso.

Geisel, Ernesto.
President of Brazil, 1974-. Career military officer. Born 3 August 1908. Entered army 31 March 1925; advanced to rank of general 25 March 1961. Attended Army Command and General Staff College, Fort Leavenworth, Kansas. Longtime member of National Petroleum Council. Former superintendent of President Bernardes oil refinery. Chief of military cabinet and secretary-general of National Security Council in Castello Branco government, 1964-1967. Minister of Military Supreme Court, 1967-1969. President of Petrobrás, 1969-1973.

Geisel, Orlando.
Minister of the Army, 1969-1974. Career army officer. Born 5 September 1905. Entered army 23 February 1923; advanced to rank of General of the Army, 25 November 1965. Brother of President Ernesto Geisel.

Gomes, Emílio.
Governor of Paraná, 1971-.

Gómez, Severo.
Minister of Industry and Commerce, 1974-. Minister of Agriculture in Castello Branco government, 1964-1967.

Gonsalves, Wilson.
ARENA senator from Ceará. First vice president of the Senate, 1970-.

Guilhon, Fernando.
Governor of Pará, 1971-. President of Docks of Pará Company, 1970.

Guimarães, Ulysses Silveira.
Civilian politician. Federal deputy from São Paulo for the opposition Brazilian Democratic Movement (MDB). MDB candidate for the presidency of Brazil, 1973.

Henning, Geraldo de Azevedo.
Career naval officer. An admiral. Minister of the Navy, 1974-.

Krieger, Daniel.
ARENA senator from Rio Grande do Sul. Born 10 April 1909 in São Nicolau, Rio Grande do Sul. Took part in revolutions of 1930 and 1964. Represented governments of Jânio Quadros, Castello Branco, and Costa e Silva in the Senate, 1961-1969. First president of ARENA.

Lages, Afranio.
Governor of Alagoas, 1971-.

Lagoa, Francisco de Paula da Rocha.
Minister of Health, 1969-1974.

Leite, Eraldo Gueiros.
Governor of Pernambuco, 1971. Former justice on Supreme Military Tribunal.

Levi, Edmundo Fernandes.
Senator from Amazonas for the opposition Brazilian Democratic Movement (MDB). Elected third secretary of the Senate, 1970.

Lima, Affonso Augusto Albuquerque.
Career army officer. Born in Ceará, 22 August 1909. Entered army 1 April 1927; promoted to general 25 July 1964. Minister of Interior, March 1967-January 1969. Supported by young nationalist officers in unsuccessful bid for the presidency in 1969. Retired 1970.

Lima, Evando de Souza.
Career military officer. A general. Superintendent of the Superintendency for the Development of the Northeast (SUDENE), 1969-1974.

Lima, Luís Fernando Cirne.
Minister of Agriculture, 1969-1974.

Lima Sobrinho, Alexandre José Barbosa.
Prominent Brazilian writer. Born 1897. Member of opposition Brazilian Democratic Movement (MDB). Its candidate for the vice presidency of Brazil, 1973.

Lorscheider, (Dom) Aloísio.
President of the National Conference of Brazilian Bishops.

Macedo, Joelmo Campos de Araripe.
Career air force officer. Brigadier general. Minister of Air, 1969-, serving under both Médici and Geisel.

Macelo, Flávio.
ARENA federal deputy and President of Chamber of Deputies.

Machado, Paulo de Almeida.
Minister of Health in Geisel government, 1974-. President of Instituto Nacional de Pesquisas da Amazônia, 1973-1974. A physician.

Madureira, Horâcio.
Director general of National Department of Railroads (DNEF).

Magalhães, Antônio Carlos.
Civilian politician. Governor of Bahia, 1971-. Former mayor of Salvador.

Magalhães Pinto, José de.
ARENA senator from Minas Gerais. Born 19 March 1908 at Santo Antônio do Monte, Minas Gerais. President of National Democratic Union (UDN) party in 1959. Governor of Minas Gerais, 1960-1965. Suggested as Prime Minister in 1961. First governor to lead his state in rebellion against Goulart, March 1964. Foreign Minister in Costa e Silva government, 1967-1969.

Mattos, Juvenal.
Senator of the opposition Brazilian Democratic Movement (MDB) from São Paulo. Elected second vice president of the Senate, 1970.

Médici, Emílio Garrastazu.
President of Brazil, 1969-1974. Born 4 December 1905 at Bagé, Rio Grande do Sul. Entered military 1 April 1924; advanced to rank of general on 25 July 1961. Commander of Agulhas Negras Military Academy at time of revolution in 1964. Military attaché in Washington, 1964-1966. Head of National Information Service (SNI) under Costa e Silva, 1967-1969. Was Commander of the Third Army in Rio Grande do Sul when he was selected to succeed Costa e Silva in the presidency, October 1969.

Mello, Márcio de Souza.
Career air force officer, a marshal. Air Minister, 1969-1974. Born in Santa Catarina in 1906. Member of military junta, August-October 1969.

Moraes, Marcus Vinícius Pratini de.
Minister of Industry and Commerce, 1969-1974.

Natel, Laudo.
Governor of São Paulo, 1971-. He was vice governor in 1966 when Governor Adhemar de Barros was removed from office. Served out the balance of de Barros' term.

Nogueira, Dirceu de Araújo.
Career army officer, a general. Minister of Transportation, 1974-. Served in Directorate of Engineering and Communications in Army Ministry during the Médici government, 1969-1974. Past military commander of Amazonas.

Nunes, Adalberto de Barros.
Career naval officer, an admiral. Minister of the Navy, 1969-1974.

Oliveira, Araken de.
Career army officer, a general. President of National Petroleum Council.

Oliveira, Euclides Quandt de.
Career naval officer, a commandant. Minister of Communications in Geisel government, 1974-.

Pacheco, Rondon.
Civilian politician. Governor of Minas Gerais, 1971-. Born 31 July 1919 in Uberlândia, Minas Gerais. Studied law at University of Minas Gerais. Former congressman of National Democratic Union (UDN) party. Head of Civil Household of presidency, 1967-1969.

Padilha, Raimundo Delmiriano.
Civilian politician. Governor of Rio de Janeiro, 1971-. Former congressman of National Democratic Union (UDN) party, 1954-1965.

Pamplona, Confúcio.
Career military officer, a colonel. Secretary-general of Ministry of Education and Culture, 1969-1974.

Passarinho, Jarbas Gonçalves.
Minister of Education and Culture in Médici government, 1969-1974. Born 11 January 1920. Minister of Labor, 1967-1969. Army major.

Pécora, José Flávio.
Secretary-general of Ministry of Finance, 1969-1974.

Pedrossian, Pedro.
Civilian politician. Governor of Mato Grosso, 1966-1970. Past executive director of Northwest Railroad.

Pereira, Cortez.
Governor of Rio Grande do Norte, 1971-. Former director of Bank of the Northeast. Former state deputy.

Peres, Haroldo Leon.
Governor of Paraná, 1966-1970. Civilian politician. Former state deputy of National Democratic Union (UDN) party.

Pimentel, Paulo.
Governor of Paraná, 1971-. Civilian politician. Former federal deputy of Social Democratic Party (PSD).

Portela, Petrônio.
ARENA senator from Piauí. ARENA president in Senate. Past governor of Piauí. Toured Brazil for presidential candidate, Ernesto Geisel, 1973.

Prieto, Arnaldo da Costa.
Minister of Labor, 1974-. Born in São Francisco de Paulo, Rio Grande do Sul. Past federal deputy, ARENA leader. Former secretary of labor in Rio Grande do Sul.

Rademaker Grünewald, Augusto Hamann.
Vice President of Brazil, 1969-1974. Career naval officer, an admiral. Active in 1964 revolution. Member of Revolutionary High Command, 1964. Minister of Navy, 1967-1969. Member of military junta, August-October 1969.

Rêgo, Gustavo Morais.
Career military officer, a colonel. Special advisor to President Geisel.

Rêgo, José Tavares Bordeaux.
Career air force officer. Chief of Department of Civil Aviation in Médici government, 1969-1974.

Reis, Maurício Rangel.
Minister of Interior in Geisel government, 1974-.

Rio Branco, Miguel do.
Ambassador to Israel, November 1973-.

Sá, Ângelo.
President of Bank of Brazil, 1974-. Past superintendent of Bank of Bahia.

Salgado, Plínio.
Civilian politician. ARENA federal deputy from São Paulo. Born at São Bento do Sapucaí, São Paulo, 22 January 1901. Organizer and leader of the neo-fascist Brazilian Integralist Action party, 1932-1938. Exiled to Portugal, 1938-1948. Organizer and leader of Party of Popular Representation (PRP), and its presidential candidate in 1955.

Salles, Colombo.
Governor of Santa Catarina, 1971-.

Santana, Pedro Neivas de.
Governor of Maranhão, 1971-. Ex-secretary of finance, Maranhão and past rector of the University of Maranhão.

Santos, Adalberto Pereira dos.
Vice President of Brazil, 1974-. Career army officer, a general. Born 11 April 1905. Entered military service 1 April 1924; attained rank of General of the Army 25 November 1965. Attended Armored Infantry School in United States.

Santos, Arthur Gerhardt dos.
Governor of Espírito Santo, 1971-.

Santos, Rui.
Civilian politician. ARENA senator from Bahia. First secretary of the Senate. Former federal deputy of National Democratic Union (UDN) party.

Sátiro, Ernani.
Civilian politician. Governor of Paraíba, 1971-. Former federal deputy of National Democratic Union (UDN) party.

Silveira, Antônio Francisco Azeredo da.
Career diplomat. Foreign Minister, 1974-. Ambassador to Argentina, 1973-1974.

Silveira, Hélio Prates de.
Governor of Federal District, 1971-. Career military officer, a colonel.

Simonsen, Mário Henrique.
Finance Minister, 1974-. Born 19 February 1935 at Rio de Janeiro. Graduate from National Engineering School, 1957, and from University of Rio de Janeiro, 1963. Lecturer at Getúlio Vargas Foundation, 1961-. Vice President of Bozzano Bank. Former adviser to the president of the National Confederation of Industry. Member of administrative council of National Housing Bank. Financial consultant to Mercedes Benz do Brasil, Santos Docks Company, and Souza Cruz Cigarette Company.

Tauney, Jorge d'Escragnolle.
Career diplomat. Ambassador to Lebanon, 1974-. Chief of protocol of the presidency, 1969-1974.

Tavares, Aurélio de Lyra.
Army Minister, 1967-1969. Career army officer. Born in João Pessoa, Paraíba, 7 November 1905. Bachelor of Law, writer, geopolitician. Entered military service 23 February 1923; attained rank of general of the army, 25 November 1964. Head of military junta, August-October 1969. Ambassador to France, 1969-1974.

Tavares e Silva, Alberto.
Civilian politician. Governor of Piauí, 1971-.

Triches, Euclides.
Governor of Rio Grande do Sul, 1971-.

Ueki, Shigeaki.
Minister of Mines and Energy in Geisel government, 1974-. Financial director of Petrobrás, 1973.

Vieira, Laerte Ramos.
Federal deputy of the opposition Brazilian Democratic Movement (MDB) from Santa Catarina. Civilian politician. A national leader of the MDB in 1974. Former congressman of the National Democratic Union (UDN) party.

Chile

Compiled by
Richard R. Super
Lecturer in History
Arizona State University

Aguirre Doolan, Humberto.
Veteran Christian Democratic Senator. Born in Magallanes, August 1, 1908. In 1930 obtained a degree in agricultural engineering. The nephew of President Pedro Aguirre Cerda (1938-1941), he served his uncle as personal secretary. Minister of Agriculture (1946) and Lands and Colonization (1947) under President Gabriel González Videla. Elected Deputy from 1949-1953. Elected Senator, 1953-73. Vice-President of the Senate, 1973.

Alessandri Rodríguez, Jorge.
President of Chile from 1958-64. Born in Santiago, May 19, 1896. Obtained degree and faculty position from the School of Engineering in 1919. Elected Deputy from 1926-1930. President of the Paper and Carton Manufacturing Company in Puente Alto. Minister of Finance in 1947 under President Gabriel González Videla. Elected Senator from 1956-58. Elected President of Chile from 1958-64. His administration attempted measures to stabilize prices and wages in partially successful effort to halt Chile's endemic inflation. As presidential nominee of the conservative National Party, lost the 1970 election to Salvador Allende by a narrow margin.

Allende Gossens, Salvador.
President of Chile from 1970-1973. Born in Valparaíso, July 26, 1908. As student leader, participated in the downfall of President Carlos Ibáñez del Campo (1931). Twice imprisoned, once exiled, for political activities.

Graduated from the University of Chile with a medical degree in 1932. Prominent in founding Socialist Party in 1933. Elected Deputy from 1937-39. Minister of Health under President Pedro Aguirre Cerda from 1939-1941. Wrote *La realidad médico-social chilena* in 1939. Elected Senator four times from 1945-1970. President of the Senate from 1968-1969. After unsuccessful presidential campaigns in 1952, 1958, and 1964, won the presidency in 1970 supported mostly by the Communist-Socialist alliance. His Popular Unity government ended abruptly with his violent death during the military revolt of September 11, 1973. Already a leftist legend comparable to Ernesto "Che" Guevara; certainly will have a continued impact on national politics, posthumously.

Almeyda Medina, Clodomiro.
First Vice-President of outlawed Socialist Party. Foremost advisor-associate of President Salvador Allende (1970-1973). Born in Santiago, July 26, 1923. Socialist youth leader. Graduated from the University of Chile with a law degree. From 1952-1953, Minister of Labor and Mines under President Carlos Ibáñez del Campo. Elected Deputy from 1961-1965. Long-time member of the Central Committee of the Socialist Party. Co-owner of the now-banned Socialist daily, *La Ultima Hora.* Served in every Allende Cabinet from 1970-1973, mostly as Minister of Foreign Affairs. As Vice-President of the Socialist Party from 1971-1973, supported the relatively moderate Allende position within the party against the extremist majority who demanded more rapid and radical change. Arrested and imprisoned by the military following the September 11, 1973 coup.

Altamirano Orrego, Carlos.
Secretary-General of the outlawed Socialist Party. Senator. Lawyer. Elected Deputy from 1961-1965. Twice elected Senator from 1965-1973. At the Socialists' National Convention of February, 1971, named the Secretary-General of the PS. Representing the extremist majority within the party, constantly pushed President Salvador Allende to undertake more radical programs of agrarian reform, nationalization of industries, and politico-military purges. His attempt to foment a naval mutiny in August, 1973 has been cited by the military as the immediate provocation of the September 11, 1973 coup. Following the revolt, was one of the most-hunted leftists by the ruling junta. Rumored to have fled to Havana, Cuba.

Aylwin Azocar, Patricio.
President of the Christian Democratic Party. Senator. Born in Viña del Mar, 1918. Graduated from the University of Chile with a law degree in 1944. President of the National Falange in 1951. Three times President of the PDC: 1958-1960, 1965, 1973. Twice elected Senator from 1965-1973. In August, 1973 participated in series of face-to-face dialogues with President Salvador Allende in a final, fruitless attempt to secure a *modus viven-*

di between the deadlocked Executive and Congressional branches of government.

Benavides Escobar, César Raúl.

Army General. Minister of Interior under the military junta since July, 1974. Born in 1919. Commissioned in 1938. In August, 1973 Director of Army Operations when appointed commandant of all military institutes. During military coup of September 11, 1973 played key role as field commander of one of two "Santiago operational commands"; directed East Group with primary objective the occupation of Tomás Moro, Allende's private residence. Commanding officer of Army Fifth Division in Punta Arenas and Intendant of Magallanes from December, 1973-July, 1974.

Bonilla Bradanovic, Oscar.

Army General. Minister of National Defense under the military junta since July, 1974. Aide-de-camp to President Eduardo Frei. Active in suppressing the tank commander's revolt against Allende's government on June 29, 1973. Close friend of pro-Allende Commander-in-Chief General Carlos Prats González until dispute in late August, 1973. Participated in the military coup of September 11, 1973. Minister of Interior from September 1973-July 1974.

Bossay Leyva, Luis.

Veteran Radical Party Congressman. Born in Valparaíso, December 3, 1912. Student leader in his hometown. President of Radical Assembly of Valparaíso and president of the first PR Youth Convention in 1939. Elected Deputy three times from 1941-1953. Named to various Cabinet posts by President Gabriel González Videla. In 1958, lost a bid for the presidency under the PR banner. Elected three times to the Senate from 1953-1973. Congressman commanding the most seniority by 1973. Senate Vice-President in 1973. In July, 1973, led a movement to re-unite the fractured PR by merging three Radical sects into the new Chilean Social Democratic Party.

Briones Olivos, Carlos.

Twice Minister of Interior under President Salvador Allende. Born in San Carlos, November 4, 1915. Graduated from the University of Chile with a law degree in 1953. Career in private practice and as legal advisor to various governmental agencies. Personal friend of Salvador Allende. Moderate Socialist. Appointed Superintendent of Social Security after 1970. In July, 1973, President Allende named him Minister of Interior apparently with the mission to seek some compromise with the Christian Democrats. The dialogue which he arranged between President Allende and Senator Aylwin had little lasting effect. Minister of Interior when military revolted on September 11, 1973.

Carmona Peralta, Juan de Dios.

Prominent Christian Democratic Senator. Born in Antofagasta,

December 22, 1916. Regional and student leader in the National Falange. Law degree in 1944. City official in Antofagasta from 1947-1949. Elected Deputy three times from 1949-1961. Vice-President of the Chamber of Deputies. Minister of National Defense for President Eduardo Frei from 1964-1968. Elected Senator in 1969. Authored crucial Arms Control Law of 1972. Enforcement of that bill by the armed forces in 1973 apparently convinced military leaders that the Allende government was arming workers against them.

Carvajal Prado, Patricio.

Vice-Admiral. Minister of Foreign Affairs under the military junta since July, 1974. Born in Santiago, September 13, 1916. Obtained naval commission in 1935. By 1956, promoted to Frigate Captain and to the Naval Staff. Training in anti-submarine tactics in the United States, 1958. In 1962, Director of the Navy's Artillery School. Naval Attaché to Great Britain in 1964. By the September 11, 1973 revolt, Chief of Staff of the Chilean Armed Forces. Minister of National Defense from September, 1973-July, 1974.

Castro Jiménez, Hugo.

Rear-Admiral. Minister of Public Education under the military junta since September, 1973. Born in Valparaíso, 1922. Administrator with the Office of Naval Education from 1954-1955. Expert in torpedo warfare. Director of the Naval Academy from 1971-1972. As Education Minister, has abolished the traditional autonomous status of Chilean universities and restructured much of the educational system in Chile.

Cauas Lama, Jorge.

Civil Engineer. Economist. Minister of Finance under the military junta since July, 1974. Born in San Felipe, August 13, 1934. Engineering studies at Columbia University of New York and the University of Chile. Accepted United States government scholarship for graduate studies in the United States from 1960-1961. Professor at the University of Chile. Vice-President of the Central Bank from 1967-1970 and May-July 1974. Founder and director of World Bank's Department of Studies from October, 1973-May, 1974.

Corvalán Lépez, Luis.

Secretary-General of the outlawed Chilean Communist Party. Born in 1916. Schoolteacher. Labor leader. Journalist. Editor of the Communist daily, *El Siglo*. Elected Senator from 1961-1969. PCCh Secretary-General from 1958-1973. A consistent advocate of the "peaceful road" policy. Joined his party with the Socialists to elect Salvador Allende in 1970. Obviously very influential in the Popular Unity government from 1970-1973. Arrested and imprisoned by the military following the September 11, 1973 coup.

Díaz Estrada, Nicanor.
Air Force Brigadier General. Minister of Labor under the military junta since July, 1974.

Ewing Hodar, Pedro.
Army Colonel. Government Secretary-General under the military junta since September, 1973. Born in 1927. Son of Army Colonel Alfredo Ewing who participated in the military junta that ousted President Arturo Alessandri in September, 1924. Artillery specialist. Professor of geopolitics.

Figueroa Gutiérrez, Sergio.
Air Force General. Minister of Public Works under the military junta since September, 1973.

Frei Montalva, Eduardo.
President of Chile from 1964-1970. Christian Democratic Senator. President of the Senate. Born in Santiago, January 16, 1911. Graduated from the University of Chile with a law degree in 1933. Editor of the Iquique daily *El Tarapacá* in 1934. Active in the founding of the National Falange. Professor of labor law at the University of Chile in 1937. Author of many works of political philosophy, including *La verdad tiene su hora,* for which he won the National Literary Award in 1956. Minister of Public Works under President Juan Antonio Ríos in 1945 and 1946. Twice elected Senator from 1949-1964. Unsuccessful presidential candidate in 1958. Won the presidency in 1964. Administration marked by programs of gradual agrarian reform and greater control over the copper industry. Elected Senator in 1973. The most probable civilian successor to President Salvador Allende at the time of the military revolt of September 11, 1973.

Garín Cea, Enrique.
Army Brigadier General, Retired. Minister of Transportation under the military junta. Born in 1919. Artillery officer. Military Attaché to Venezuela. Assistant director of the Military Academy. Commandant of all military institutes. Professor of logistics and tactics in War College. Since September 11, 1973 coup advisor to military junta on transportation and mass transit. Appointed to newly-created cabinet post in July, 1974.

González Videla, Gabriel.
President of Chile from 1946-1952. Born in La Serena, November 22, 1898. Law degree from the University of Chile in 1922. Elected Deputy three times from 1930-1939. President of the Radical Party and promoter of the Chilean Popular Front in 1938. Ambassador to France from 1939-1941. Ambassador to Brazil from 1942-1944. Elected Senator in 1945. Elected President in 1946. Appointed first Communists to Cabinet posts in 1946. Outlawed Communist Party and severed relations with the Soviet

Union in 1948. Granted women's suffrage for national elections in 1949. In 1970 waged an unsuccessful campaign to re-unite the split PR.

Herrera Latoja, Francisco.

Air Force General, retired. Minister of Public Health under the military junta since July, 1974. Born in Talcahuano, October 22, 1920. Attended Military Academy and received special electronic communications training in the United States. Army commission in 1941. Air Force commission in 1958. Attended United States officers' schools in 1958. Secretary to Air Force Attaché to the United States in 1961. Specialist in telecommunications.

Huerta Díaz, Ismael.

Rear Admiral. Ambassador to the United Nations under the military junta since July, 1974. Minister of Public Works under President Salvador Allende in early 1973. Minister of Foreign Relations from September, 1973-July, 1974.

Huidobro Justiniano, Sergio.

Admiral. Commander of the Chilean Marine Corps. Born in Santiago, December 25, 1921. Graduated from the Naval Academy with a commission in the Coast Guard in 1942. From 1955-1956, took United States Marine training courses at Quantico and Norfolk, Virginia. Director of Studies at the Coast Guard School in 1956. Enrolled in the Naval War College from 1959-1960. Graduated with specialized degrees in marine infantry and amphibious operations. Professor at the Naval War College. Aide to Navy Commander-in-Chief Admiral José Toribio Merino.

Jarpa Reyes, Sergio Onofre.

President of the National Party. Senator. Born in Rengo, March 8, 1921. Landowner-businessman. Manager of a Cadillac-Cesna importing firm, then of South American Air Lines. Founder and president of National Action in 1963. Elected Senator in 1973. Led the most bitter opposition to the Allende Administration.

Leigh Guzmán, Gustavo.

Air Force General. Commander-in-Chief of the Chilean Air Force. Member of the four-man military junta. Born in Santiago, September 19, 1920. Graduated from the Air Force Academy with a commission in 1940. Promoted to lieutenant in 1944, to captain in 1949. Chief pilot for President Gabriel González Videla from 1949-1952. Received helicopter training in the United States from 1952-1953. In 1960, earned a special commendation from President Jorge Alessandri for his helicopter group's civic action work. Appointed by President Salvador Allende as Air Force Commander-in-Chief on August 17, 1973 after the controversial resignation of General César Ruiz Danyau. Participated directly in the military revolt against the Allende government on September 11, 1973 by ordering

Air Force jets to bomb the Presidential Palace. Officially assumed co-legislative powers in July, 1974.

Leighton Guzmán, Bernardo.

Prominent Christian Democratic Congressman. Born in Nascimiento, August 16, 1909. Law degree in 1933. President of Conservative Youths. Co-founder of the National Falange. Minister of Labor under President Arturo Alessandri in 1937. Elected Deputy from 1945-1949. Minister of Public Education under President Gabriel González Videla from 1950-1952. Minister of Interior under President Eduardo Frei from 1964-1968. Twice elected Deputy from 1969-1973. An influential figure in the PDC. In October, 1974 deprived of citizenship and forbidden by the military junta to re-enter Chile due to critical speeches he delivered abroad.

Léniz Cerda, Fernando.

Engineer. University professor. Minister of Economy under the military junta since September, 1973. Born in Concepción, July 30, 1927. Graduated from the University of Chile with a degree in civil engineering in 1949. Engineer for, later manager of, the Paper and Carton Manufacturing Company. An advocate of developing the nation's forest lands which he calls "Chile's green gold." One of three civilians serving in the junta's Cabinet.

McKay Jaraquemada, Mario.

Carabinero General. Minister of Lands under the military junta since July, 1974. Minister of Labor from September, 1973-July, 1974.

Mendoza Durán, César.

Carabinero General. Director General of Carabineros. Member of the four-man military junta. Graduated from the Carabinero Academy with a commission in 1940. Gained fame by winning a silver medal in equestrian events at the 1952 Olympic Games in Helsinki, Finland. During career served in numerous small Chilean towns as well as Valparaíso, Concepción, and Santiago. Named to the national police force's top post in September, 1973. Participated in the military revolt against the government of Salvador Allende on September 11, 1973. Officially assumed co-legislative powers in July, 1974.

Merino Castro, José Toribio.

Admiral. Commander-in-Chief of the Chilean Navy. Member of the four-man military junta. Born in La Serena, December 14, 1915. Graduated from the Naval Academy with a commission in 1936. Served with the United States fleet patrolling the Panama Canal Zone during World War II. Took courses in the Naval War College from 1954-1955. Professor of logistics and geopolitics. Naval Attaché to Great Britain from 1956-1957. Taught in the Naval War College from 1960-1961. Assistant Chief of the Naval Staff in 1964. Vice-Admiral by 1973. Commander of the Navy's First Zone (Valparaíso) where a leftist-inspired mutiny plot was allegedly discovered in early August, 1973. Three weeks later, succeeded Admiral Raúl Montero Cornejo as the Navy's Commander-in-Chief. Initiated the September 11 revolt against President Salvador Allende by ordering Marines to militarily occupy Valparaíso. Within the junta, apparently possesses overall responsibility for decisions concerning the nation's economy. Officially assumed co-legislative powers in July, 1974.

Musante Romero, Hugo.

Carabinero General. Minister of Justice under the military junta since July, 1974.

Olguín Zapata, Osvaldo.

Senator. First Vice-President of the Christian Democratic Party. Born in Calle Larga, 1933. Graduated from the University of Chile with a medical degree. Doctor and city official in Calama. Elected Senator in 1969. Three times named Vice-President of the PDC from 1970-1973. Participated in the face-to-face dialogues between his party and President Salvador Allende in July, 1973.

Ortúzar Escobar, Enrique.

Lawyer. President of the Constitutional Commission. Born in Santiago, November 7, 1914. Legal advisor to various Senate committees. Under President Jorge Alessandri, served as Minister of Interior, Government Secretary-General, Minister of Foreign Affairs, and Minister of Justice. Following the military coup of September 11, 1973 named president of the nine-member Constitutional Commission directed to revise the Chilean constitution.

Pinochet Ugarte, Augusto.

Army General. Commander-in-Chief of the Chilean Armed Forces. Supreme Chief of State with all rights and duties of a traditional constitutional president. Also co-legislator with other three junta members. Born in Valparaíso, November 25, 1915. Graduated from the Military Academy with a commission in 1936. Promoted to 1st lieutenant in 1942. Instructor in the Military Academy. Took courses in the Army War College from 1949-1952 to become an Army Staff officer. Promoted to major in 1953. Assigned to Rancagua Regiment in Arica. Professor in Army War College in 1954. Military Attaché to Ecuador, then to the United States, in 1956. Commanding officer of the Seventh Infantry Regiment "Esmeralda" in Antofagasta in 1961. Assistant Director and Professor of geopolitics and military geography at Army War College in 1964. Promoted to colonel in 1966. Author of various books on geopolitics and geography, one of which is an approved high school text. Training tours to the United States Southern Command in the Panama

Canal Zone in 1965, 1968, and 1972. Toured the United States in 1968 as a guest of the United States government. By 1973, Army Chief of Staff. As commander of the Buin Artillery Regiment, was active in suppressing the tank commander's revolt against the Allende government on June 29, 1973. Replaced General Carlos Prats González as Armed Forces Commander-in-Chief on August 24, 1973. Coordinated and directed the military revolt against President Salvador Allende on September 11, 1973. As presiding officer of the four-man military junta *de facto* chief executive when position formalized in July, 1974.

Prieto Gándara, Gonzalo.
Lawyer. Born in Valparaíso, June 12, 1924. Son of Naval Judge Advocate Admiral Osvaldo Prieto Castro. Graduated from the Catholic University with a law degree in 1950. Career as a civilian legal advisor for the Chilean Navy. Member of the Constitutional Commission. Minister of Justice under the military junta from September, 1973-July, 1974.

Sáez Sáez, Raúl.
Civil Engineer. Economist. Author. Minister of Economic Coordination under the military junta since July, 1974. Born in Concepción, February 16, 1913. Studied in France and Germany. Graduated from the University of Chile with engineering degree in 1938. Various positions with National Electricity Company (ENDESA) from 1952-1965; including general manager from 1961-1965. Vice-President of Chilean Development Corporation (CORFO) from 1965-1968. Minister of Finance under President Eduardo Frei in 1968. During Allende administration economic advisor to government of Venezuela. Chief economic advisor of military junta since September 11, 1973 coup. As Minister of Economic Coordination, assumed newly-created cabinet post with responsibility to coordinate activities of Planification Office (ODEPLAN) and Ministries of Finance, Economy, Agriculture and Mines.

Spoerer Covarrubias, Alberto.
Air Force Colonel. Born in Santiago, June 20, 1926. Attended both the University of Chile and Catholic University Medical Schools. Graduated with a medical degree in 1951. Commissioned into the Air Force Medical Corps. Minister of Public Health under the military junta from September 1973-July 1974.

Teitelboim Volosky, Volodia Valentín.
Communist Senator. Born in Chillán, March 17, 1916. Graduated from the University of Chile with a law degree. Journalist. Author of numerous books and essays on politics but probably best-known for novel *Hijo del salitre* (1952). Joined the Communist youth group in 1932. Member of the PCCh Central Committee. Suffered imprisonment and exile during the

party's outlawed period from 1948-1958. Well-travelled. Invited to Moscow with Pablo Neruda to attend the Second Congress of Soviet Writers in 1954. Elected Deputy from 1961-1965. Twice elected Senator from 1965-1973. Possibly the most influential Chilean Communist next to Secretary-General Luis Corvalán. Fled Chile after coup of September 11, 1973. Military junta taking action in late 1974 to deprive him of citizenship.

Tomic Romero, Radomiro.

Christian Democratic nominee for president in 1970. Born in Antofagasta, May 7, 1914. Graduated from the University of Chile with a law degree. Co-founder of the National Falange in 1935. Editor of the Iquique daily *El Tarapacá* from 1937-1941. Twice elected Deputy from 1941-1949. Elected Senator from 1949-1953. President of the National Falange in 1946 and 1952. Professor in University of Chile summer schools from 1957-1959. Chilean representative at international Christian Democratic conferences in São Paulo (1957) and Brussels (1958). Elected Deputy from 1961-1965. Appointed Ambassador to the United States by President Eduardo Frei from 1965-1968. His third-place showing in the 1970 presidential elections severely damaged his prestige within the PDC. Still remains a figure of considerable status. In late November, 1973 denied rumors that he was forming a group of leftist Christian Democrats to pressure the military into scheduling elections soon.

Toro Dávila, Agustín.

Army Brigadier General. Minister of Mines under the military junta since July, 1974.

Troncoso Daroch, Arturo.

Rear-Admiral. Minister of Housing and Urban Planning under the military junta since July, 1974.

Valdés Subercaseaux, Gabriel.

Prominent Christian Democrat. Born in Santiago, July 3, 1919. Graduated from the Catholic University with a law degree in 1945. Admitted to the Law Faculty of the Catholic University in 1954. Minister of Foreign Affairs under President Eduardo Frei from 1964-1970. At the time of September 11, 1973 military coup, Assistant Secretary-General for the United Nations with responsibility for economic development programs in Latin America. Initial rumors suggested the military junta would name him Provisional President of Chile.

Vallejos, Tucapel.

Carabinero General. Minister of Agriculture under the military junta since July, 1974.

Viveros Ávila, Arturo.

Army General. Born in Maule, 1920. Cavalry officer. Professor of logistics and military intelligence at the Army War College. Commanding officer of the Armored Division at Valdivia. Directed support groups during the military revolt against President Salvador Allende on September 11, 1973. Minister of Housing and Urban Planning under the military junta from September 1973-July 1974.

Willoughby-MacDonald Moya, Federico.
Journalist. Press Chief under the military junta since September, 1973. Born in Santiago, February 2, 1938. Studied at the University of Chile, the University of Montevideo, the University of Texas, and Chile's College of Journalism from which he graduated in 1962. Correspondent for newspapers in both Chile and the United States. Delegate to various international conferences of journalists. Secretary-General of Conservative Youths from 1959-1960.

Colombia

Compiled by
Rand Dee Bowerman
Research Associate
Center for Latin-American
Studies
Arizona State University

Aramburu, Mario.
Attorney General 1966-70.

Azuero Manchola, Rafael.
Vice-President 1973-74. Member of the Liberal Party and the Frente Nacional. Member of the Chamber of Deputies 1966-73.

Barco, Virgillio.
Executive Director IBRD, IFC, and IDA 1969-. Born 1921 in Bolivar District. Received Doctorate from MIT in Economics. Member of the Chamber of Deputies 1949-51, and of the Senate 1958-66. Minister of Public Works 1958-61. Ambassador to the United Kingdom 1961-62. Minister of Agriculture 1963-64. Mayor of Bogotá 1966-69.

Duarte Arías, Hermes.
Presidential candidate of the Christian Democratic Party (PDC) in 1974.

Echeverría Mejía, Hernán.
Leader of the Marxist National Union of Opposition (UNO). Terrorist and guerilla.

García Peña, Roberto.
Journalist. Secretary-General of the Ministry of Foreign Affairs 1938-40. Member of the Council of Directors, Inter-American Press Association.

Gómez Hurtado, Álvaro.
1974 Presidential candidate and leader of the Conservative Party of Colombia.

Holguín Sardi, Carlos.
Minister of Communications 1973-74. Chairman of the Council. Organization of American States (OAS) 1968-72.

Lleras Camargo, Alberto.
President of Colombia 1946-47 and 1958-62, Lawyer; received Law Degree from the National University of Bogotá. Secretary-General of the Liberal Party 1929. Member of the Chamber of Deputies 1930-37, Speaker 1941-43. Member of the Senate 1943. Ambassador to the United States 1943-44, and Foreign Minister 1944-46. Secretary-General of the OAS 1948-54.

Lleras Restrepo, Carlos.
President of Colombia 1966-70. Lawyer; received Law Degree from the National University of Bogotá. Member of the Chamber of Deputies 1933-38 and the Senate 1942-50. Member of the ruling Triumvirate 1950-52. Delegate to the first United Nations Plenary 1945-46.

López Michelson, Alfonso.
President of Colombia 1974-. Lawyer; received Law Degree from Nuestro Señora del Rosario University. Member of the Chamber of Deputies 1960-62. Minister of Foreign Affairs 1968-71. Member of the Senate 1962-66. Liberal Party Candidate for President in 1962.

Mercado Raquel, José.
Leader of the Confederación de Trabajadores Colombianos (CTC).

Muñoz-Duque, Cardinal Aníbal.
Archbishop of Bogotá 1972-. Cardinal of the Roman Catholic Church 1973.

Ocampo, Jaramillo.
Agriculture Minister 1972-74. Leader in the Conservative Party; lost Presidential nomination in 1974.

Ospina Pérez, Mariano.
Leader in the Conservative Party; sought Presidential nomination in 1974 and lost.

Pastrana Borrero, Misael.
President of Colombia 1970-74. Lawyer; received degree from the Pontífica Universidad Javierana. Minister of Development 1960, Minister of Public Works 1961, Minister of Finance 1961, and Minister of the Interior 1966-68. Ambassador to the United States, Delegate to the

United Nations, Delegate to the OAS, and Secretary-General of the Ministry of Foreign Affairs 1968-69. Last candidate of the Frente Nacional that ruled Colombia 1958-74.

Rojas de Moreno Díaz, María Eugenia.
Candidate for President in 1974 for the Alianza Popular Nacional (ANAPO). Member of the Senate 1970-74 and Majority Leader of the Bogota City Council 1970-74. Founder of the ANAPO in 1962. Daughter of former dictator Gustavo Rojas Pinilla.

Rojas Pinilla, Gustavo.
Dictator of Colombia 1953-57. Army officer; received training at the National Military Academy in Bogotá. Commander-in-Chief of the Armed Forces. Minister of Communications 1952. Leader in the ANAPO and its unsuccessful candidate for President 1970. Died at 75 on 17 January 1975.

Tubay Ayala, Julio César.
Journalist, politician, and diplomat. Attended Universities at Bogotá and Caracas. President of the Chamber of Deputies and member of the Senate. President of the Liberal Party 1958-63. Delegate to the United Nations 1958-61 and 1967-69. Vice-President of Colombia 1967-69.

Tulio, Cuevas.
Leader of the Unión de Trabajadores Colombianos (UTC).

Urrea Delgado, Emilio.
Mayor of Bogotá 1969-70.

Vásquez, Fabio.
Leader of the terrorist, Marxist National Liberation Army (ELN).

Costa Rica

Compiled by
Kenneth J. Grieb, Associate Professor of History and Coordinator of Latin American Studies, University of Wisconsin – Oshkosh

Arroyo Cordero, Edgar.
Minister of Government of the Republic of Costa Rica commencing in 1974. Born in 1940 in Alajuela. Licenciado in Law from the University of Costa Rica, 1965. Alderman of the Municipality of Alajuela, 1966-1970. Deputy in the Legislative Assembly and Vice-President of the Legislative Assembly, 1970-1974.

Aguilar Bonilla, Manuel.
First Vice-President of the Republic of Costa Rica, 1970-1974. Born

May 17, 1920 in San José. Studied medicine at the National Autonomous University of Mexico and Johns Hopkins University. Doctor of Medicine degree. Has held various medical positions in Mexico and Costa Rica.

Castillo Morales, Carlos Manuel.

First Vice-President of the Republic of Costa Rica, 1974-1978, and Minister of the Presidency commencing in 1974. Born in 1931. Studies at the University of Costa Rica. Master's Degree in Agricultural Economics and Rural Sociology from the University of Tennessee, 1953. Ph.D. in Economics University of Wisconsin, 1956. Served for 10 years on the Economic Commission for Latin America (CEPAL), 1956-1966, and as Secretary General of its Commission on Economic Integration, 1966-1970. Minister of Economics, Industry and Commerce, 1971-1972, at which time he resigned to participate in the Electoral campaign of Daniel Oduber Quirós.

Charpantier Gamboa, Mario.

Minister of Security of the Republic of Costa Rica commencing in 1974. Born March 15, 1933. Graduate of the Military Academy of El Salvador, 1956. Studies in Engineering in Argentina. Costa Rican Consul in Puerto Rico, 1962-1963. Costa Rican Consul in El Salvador, 1964-1965. Deputy in the Legislative Assembly, 1966-1970. Costa Rican Ambassador in El Salvador, 1970-1973. Elected a Deputy in the Legislative Assembly in the 1974 election, but resigned his seat to enter the Cabinet.

Echandi, Mario.

President of Costa Rica, 1958-1962. Candidate of the National Unification Party for the presidential term 1970-1974. Born June 17, 1915, in San José. Secretary General of the National Union Party, 1947-1950. Costa Rican Ambassador to the United States, 1950-1951. Minister of Foreign Relations, 1951-1953. Member of the National Assembly, 1953-1958.

Facio Segreda, Gonzalo.

Minister of Foreign Relations of the Republic of Costa Rica, 1970 to the present, under the administrations of José Figueres Ferrer and Daniel Oduber Quirós. Born March 28, 1918 in San José. Licenciado in Law from the University of Costa Rica, 1941. M.A. in Comparative Jurisprudence, New York University, 1948. Professor in the School of Law at the University of Costa Rica, 1944-1951, and 1951-1962. Co-Founder of the National Liberation Party, Member of its Executive Committee, 1948-1956, Member of its Planning Committee, 1959-1962, and Member of its National Coordinating Committee, 1966-1974. Member of the Founding Junta of the Second Republic, 1948-1949. Minister of Justice and Grace of the Republic of Costa Rica, 1948. Minister of Foreign Relations, 1948-1949. Minister of the Treasury and Economy, 1949. Deputy in the National Assembly. President of the National

Assembly, 1953-1955. Has headed the Costa Rican Delegation to numerous international conferences, including several General Assemblies of the United Nations and several meetings of the Organization of American States. Costa Rican Ambassador to the United States and Costa Rican Representative to the Council of the Organization of American States, 1956-1958 and 1962-1966. President of the Council of the Organization of American States, 1962-1963. Has served as editor and columnist for various journals, and as editor of the newspaper *La República,* 1955-1956.

Figueres Ferrer, José.
President of the Republic of Costa Rica, 1970-1974, and 1953-1958. Born September 25, 1906 in San Ramón. Studies in Engineering at the Massachusetts Institute of Technology and at the National Autonomous University of Mexico. A coffee planter prior to his entry into politics in 1948. Founder and chairman of the National Liberation Party, 1948 to the present. Chairman of the Founding Junta of the Second Republic, 1958-1959. Has represented his nation at numerous international conferences and conclaves. The author of numerous newspaper and journal articles dealing with political subjects in Costa Rica and throughout Latin America.

Garrón Salazar, Hernán.
Minister of Agriculture and Dairying of the Republic of Costa Rica, commencing in 1974. Born July 3, 1917 in San José. President of the Municipality of Limón, 1953-1958. Deputy in the Legislative Assembly, 1958-1962 and 1966-1970, serving as President of the Legislative Assembly in 1967. Minister of Industry and Commerce, 1962-1964. President of the Board of Directors of the Central Bank, 1971.

González Martén, Jorge.
Presidential Candidate of the National Independent Party in the 1974 elections. Born October 3, 1926 in San José. Studied at the University of Costa Rica. Engaged in agriculture and held various administrative positions within the Ministry of the Treasury.

Jenkins Morales, Álvaro.
Minister of Transport of the Republic of Costa Rica commencing in 1974. Born in San Ramón. Mechanical Engineering Degree from Iowa State University. Also studies at Clemson University. Served in the Point Four Program of the Agency of International Development, 1952-1953. Served as an engineer for various private companies, 1954-1970.

Mora Valverde, Manuel.
Chairman of the Social Action Party and its Presidential candidate in numerous elections, including 1974. Born August 27, 1909 in San José. Licenciado in Law from the University of Costa Rica. Long time head of

the Costa Rican Communist Party, member of the National Assembly and National Congress, and frequent Presidential candidate.

Naranjo Coto, Carmen.

Minister of Culture, Youth, Sports of the Republic of Costa Rica, commencing in 1974. Born in 1930 in Cartago. Licenciado in Law, University of Costa Rica. Additional studies at the National Autonomous University of Mexico and the University of Iowa. Has held managerial positions in the Costa Rican Electrical Institute and the Costa Rican Social Security Institute, serving as Secretary General of the Costa Rican Institute of Social Security, 1961-1971. Costa Rican Ambassador to Israel, 1972-1973. Author of several novels.

Oduber Quirós, Daniel.

President of the Republic of Costa Rica, 1974-. Born August 25, 1921 in San José. Licenciado in Law from the University of Costa Rica, 1945. Master's Degree from McGill University in Montreal. Ph.D. from Sorbonne University in Paris. One of the founders and long time members of the National Liberation Party. Secretary General of the Founding Junta of the Second Republic, 1948-1949. Chief of Propaganda and Coordinator of the Investigative Commissions of the National Liberation Party, 1953. Costa Rican Ambassador in Europe, 1953-1955. Secretary General of the National Liberation Party, 1956-1958. Deputy in the National Assembly and Leader of the National Liberation Party Deputies, 1958-1962. Minister of Foreign Relations, 1962-1965. Presidential candidate of the National Liberation Party in the 1966 elections. President of the Legislative Assembly, 1970-1973. President of the National Liberation Party, 1970-1974. Author of numerous works on politics and development of Costa Rica. Elected President of the Republic of Costa Rica for the term 1974-1978, in the 1974 elections, as candidate of the National Liberation Party.

Sánchez Méndez, Jorge.

Minister of the Economy, Industry, and Commerce of the Republic of Costa Rica commencing in 1974. Born in 1934. Degree from the School of Economic and Social Sciences, 1960. Professor of Economics at the University of Costa Rica. A long time employee of the Bank of Costa Rica. Vice Minister of Economy, Industry and Commerce, 1970-1972. Minister of Economics, Industry, and Commerce, 1972-1973, at which time he resigned to participate in the electoral campaign.

Terjos Escalante, Fernándo.

Presidential candidate of the National Unification Party in the 1974 elections. Born February 27, 1927 in San José. Studies at Drew University and the National Autonomous University of Mexico. Holds a Doctorate in Medicine. Professor in the Faculty of Medicine of the University of

Costa Rica. Has held numerous administrative positions in Costa Rican hospitals and medical institutions. President of the National Association of Economic Development. Deputy in the National Assembly, 1966-1970.

Trejos Fernández, José Joaquín.

President of the Republic of Costa Rica, 1966-1970. Born April 18, 1916 in San José. Post Graduate study in Mathematics at the University of Chicago, 1946-1947. He served the University of Costa Rica as: Founding Professor and Dean of the School of Economic and Social Sciences, 1943-1965; founder of the Institute of Economic Investigation and the Institute of Statistics; Dean of the Central Faculty of Sciences and Letters, 1958-1961; Vice Rector, 1956; and University Representative on the National Superior Council of Education. Member of the Board of Directors of the Central Bank of Costa Rica, 1959-1962. Representative of the Central Bank of Costa Rica to the International Monetary Fund, Washington, 1961. Author of various works regarding education in Costa Rica, and of numerous articles in the field of economics.

Volio Jiménez, Fernando.

Minister of Public Education of the Republic of Costa Rica, commencing in 1974. Born in 1924 in Cartago. Licenciado in Law from the University of Costa Rica. Alderman of the Municipalities of Cartago and San José. Served two terms as a Deputy in the Legislative Assembly. Costa Rican Ambassador to the United Nations, serving as Vice President of the General Assembly and President on the Commission on Human Rights. Vice Minister of Youth Culture and Sports, and President of the National Council of Sports. Professor in the Faculty of Law of the University of Costa Rica. President of the Editorial Costa Rica, 1970 to the present. Author of one book and various articles. Member of the National Association of Lawyers and National Association of Authors.

Cuba

Compiled by
Joel C. Edelstein
Profesor Asistente,
Departamento de
Relaciones Internacionales
Universidad de las Américas

NOTE: The government reorganization of November 1972 established an Executive Committee of the Council of Ministers. It is composed of the Prime Minister, the President of the Republic and several Deputy Prime Ministers, each of whom is in charge of a sector which includes a number of ministries and institutes.

Following the defeat of Batista, the anti-militarism of the new government was expressed through a tradition of awarding no rank higher than that of Major in the Revolutionary Armed Forces (FAR). This practice was discontinued in December 1973 in order to provide an appropriate command structure for the more complex and technically advanced military forces which have been created and to overcome the problem of equivalency of rank in meetings between high officers of the FAR and military leaders from other nations. We have adopted the practice used in the Cuban press of listing the rank held in the FAR, followed by its international equivalent, stated in parentheses; e.g., Division Commander (Lieutenant General) Raúl Castro Ruz. The rank of Major in Cuba is now equivalent to the customary position and degree of responsibility of that rank in the command structure of military institutions in other nations. However, revolutionary leaders who earned the rank of Major during the period of armed struggle but who have not been active in the FAR since then still hold this rank. In these instances it has a meaning different from its significance if earned after December 1973.

Abrantes, José.

First Commander (Colonel), First Deputy Minister of the Ministry of the Interior. Member of the Central Committee of the Communist Party of Cuba (PCC).

Acosta, Armando.

Major. First Secretary of the Provincial Direction of Oriente of the PCC. Member of the Central Committee of the PCC.

Aguirre, Severo.

Major. Member of the Central Committee of the PCC. A leader in the Partido Socialista Popular (PSP), the Moscow-oriented Communist Party which was merged with the 26th of July Movement and the Revolutionary Directorate to form the United Party of the Socialist Revolution (PURS) in 1961.

Alarcón de Quesada, Ricardo.

Permanent representative to the United Nations, 1966-. Born in 1937. Educated at the University of Havana. Head of the Student Section, provincial office of the July 26th Movement, 1957-1959. Director of Regional Policies (Latin America), Ministry of Foreign Affairs, 1962-1966. Member of the Governing Council of the Institute for International Affairs, Ministry of Foreign Affairs.

Alfara, Carlos.

Cuban ambassador to Syria. Member of the Central Committee of the PCC.

Almeida Bosque, Juan.

Major. Army commander. Born in Havana. Bricklayer by trade. Veteran of the Moncada Attack, 1953. Jailed with Fidel Castro. Exiled to

Mexico. Member of the GRANMA's expeditionary force. First Lieutenant to Fidel in the Sierra Maestra. Cuban war hero. Member of the Political Bureau of the Central Committee of the PCC and its delegate in Oriente Province.

Amado Blanco, Luis.
Cuban ambassador to the Vatican.

Amaro, Olga.
General Secretary of the Trade Union of Workers in Education and Science.

Anillo, René.
First Deputy of Foreign Relations. Studied law at the University of Havana, was closely associated with the Directorio Revolucionario.

Aragones, Emilio.
Director of the National Institute of Fishing.

Arufe, Alberto.
Secretary of Culture, Sports, and Recreation of the Young Communist League.

Bravo Prado, Flavio.
Major. Chief of Operations of the Revolutionary Armed Forces. Deputy Prime Minister in charge of Consumer Goods Industries and Domestic Trade. Member of the PSP during the Batista Regime. Member of the Central Committee of the PCC.

Bravo Yáñez, Manuel.
First Commander (Colonel). Head of the Foreign Relations Department of the Ministry of the Revolutionary Armed Forces (FAR).

Cabrera González, Francisco.
Brigade commander (Major General). Deputy Minister and Chief of the Revolutionary Antiaircraft Defense and Air Force.

Calcines, Faustino.
Vice-Minister of Labor. Leader of PSP during the Batista period. Member of the Central Committee of the PCC.

Carcaño, Dora.
General Secretary of the Cuban Federation of Women (FMC).

Carpentier y Valmont, Alejo.
Cultural attaché of Cuba in France. Born in 1904. Educated at the University of Havana. Author of various novels and short stories including *El siglo de las luces*. Considered one of Latin America's most important novelists.

Casas Regueiro, Senén.

Brigade Commander (Major General). First Deputy Minister and Head of the General Staff of the Revolutionary Armed Forces.

Castilla Mas, Belarmino.

Deputy Prime Minister in charge of Education, Science and Culture. Member of the Central Committee of the PCC. Major in the Rebel Armed Forces during the revolutionary war.

Castro Ruz, Fidel.

Prime Minister, 1959- and Commander in Chief of the FAR, (INRA) and President of the National Institute of Agrarian Reform 1965-. Presides over the Executive Committee of the Council of Ministers (formed in 1972) and has responsibility to the Council for the Ministry of the FAR, the Ministry of the Interior, Secretariat of the Presidency and the Council of Ministers, INRA, Ministry of Public Health and the Children's Institute. Born in Oriente Province in 1926. Educated in Jesuit schools and at the University of Havana where he received his law degree. Practiced law, 1950-1952. Ran for Congress in 1952. Led the attack on Moncada Barracks on July 26, 1953. Went to the United States to raise funds in exile communities to finance the armed rebellion which he organized in Mexico. Led the GRANMA expedition to Cuba in December, 1956. Carried on an armed struggle against Batista until 1959. First Secretary of the Partido Unido de la Revolución Socialista (PURS), 1963-1965, and of the Partido Comunista de Cuba, 1965-. Has travelled to Latin America, Asia, Africa, Eastern Europe and the U.S.S.R. in his official capacity. Author of various books including *History Will Absolve Me* and *Ten Years of Revolution.* Major in militia.

Castro Ruz, Raúl.

Deputy Prime Minister, 1960-. Second Secretary of the Central Committee of the Communist Party of Cuba. Division Commander (Lieutenant General), and Minister of the Armed Forces, 1959-. Born in Oriente Province in 1930. Younger brother of Fidel Castro. Educated in Jesuit schools. Took part in the attack on the Moncada Barracks. Imprisoned for insurrection in 1953. Released in 1954. Exile in Mexico, 1954-1956. Took part in the GRANMA expedition. Assisted Fidel Castro in the Sierra Maestra. Thought to be logical successor to Fidel Castro. Spends much of his time touring the countryside "to bring the revolution closer to the people." Major in militia. Married to Vilma Espín.

Chaveco, Joel.

Minister of the Merchant Marine and Ports.

Chomón Mediavilla, Faure.

Minister of Transportation, 1963-. Born in Camagüey. Joined Castro's movement as a student. Veteran of Escambray. Leader of the attack on the presidential palace in March, 1957. Co-founder with José Echevarría of the Revolutionary Directorate. Secretary-General of the Directorio Estudiantil, 1957. Ambassador to the Soviet Union, 1960-1962. Minister of Communications, 1962-1963. Major in militia. Member of the PCC Secretariat.

Cienfuegos, Osmani.

Chairman of the Foreign Relations Committee of the PCC. Born in Havana. Younger brother of Camilo Cienfuegos. Minister of Public Works, 1959-1966. Captain in militia. Member of many delegations to other nations.

Crombet, Jaime.

Second Secretary of the PCC. Provincial Committee in Camagüey. Former First Secretary of the Young Communist League (UJC). President of the FEU in 1965.

Darias, Rubén.

Minister of Public Works, 1967-.

Darias Rodes, Ramón.

Minister of Construction, 1967-. Minister of Public Works 1965-1967.

Del Valle Jiménez, Sergio.

Minister of the Interior. Early member of the July 26th Movement. Vice Minister of the FAR. Chief of the General Staff until 1966. Appointed to the National Directorate of the ORI (Integrated Revolutionary Organization) in 1961. Member of the Political Bureau of the PCC.

Díaz, Telesforo.

Director of Information of the Cuban Ministry of Foreign Relations. Member of the Central Committee of the PCC.

Díaz González, Manuel.

Member of the Central Committee of the PCC. Head of the Foreign Relations Department of the Ministry of the FAR.

Domenech Benítez, Joel.

Deputy Prime Minister. Former Minister of Basic Industry. Minister of Industry, 1966-1967. Member of the Central Committee of the PCC.

Domínguez, Luis Orlando.

First Secretary of the National Committee of the Young Communist League (UJC).

Dorticós Torrado, Osvaldo.

President of Cuba, 1959-. Born in 1919. Law degree from the University of Havana. As a law student he was a PSP organization secretary in his home town of Cienfuegos. Leader of the 26th of July Movement in Cienfuegos, 1957-1958. Arrested and imprisoned in December 1958. Escaped to Mexico and returned after the success of the Revolution. Minister of Revolutionary Laws, January-July 1959. Also Minister of the Economy and Central Planning Board, 1964-. Vice President of the Cuban Bar Association and of the Central Committee. Responsible to the Executive Committee of the Council of Administration for the National Bank, the Ministry of Foreign Trade, the National Institute of Fishing, the Ministry of Justice and the Ministry of Labor.

Esquirel, Antonio.
Minister of Basic Industry.

Espín, Vilma.
President of the Federation of Cuban Women. Born in Santiago de Cuba. Architect from a wealthy family. Director of the attack on Santiago in November 1956. Combatant on the Second Front during the Revolution. Aide and then wife of Raúl Castro. Member of the Central Committee of the PCC.

Fernández, José R.
Minister of Education.

Fernández Font, Marcelo.
Minister of Foreign Trade, 1965-. National Organization Coordinator of the July 26th Movement and political theoretician.

Fernández Padilla, Oscar.
Minister of Labor.

Figueroa, Max.
Director of the Center of Educational Development of the Ministry of Education.

Frometa, Nora.
Minister of Light Industry.

Fundora, Orlando.
Head of the Commission of Revolutionary Orientation.

García, Juan Antonio.
Official of the Ministry of Foreign Relations. Member of the Central Committee of the PCC. Acting Director of the Cuban Ministry of Foreign Relations' Department on Asia and Africa.

García, Rigoberto.
Brigade Commander (Major General), Deputy Minister of the FAR.

García Bango, Jorge.
Director of the National Institute of Sports, Physical Education and Recreation.

García Fría, Guillermo.
Major. Deputy Prime Minister in charge of the Transportation and Communication Sector. War hero. Member of the Central Committee and the Political Bureau of the PCC. One of the first to join Castro in the Sierra Maestra. Chief of the Armed Forces of Occidente during the Revolution.

García Lazo, Hermino.
Deputy Minister of Trade Policy with Socialist Countries of the Ministry of Foreign Trade.

García Peláez, Pedro.
Brigade Commander (Major General), Chief of the Central Army of the FAR.

García Peláez, Raúl.
Ambassador to the Soviet Union, 1967-. Law degree from the University of Havana. Former member of the July 26th Revolutionary Committee. Prosecutor of Camagüey Court of Appeals. Member of the Secretariat of the Central Committee of the PCC, 1965-. Head of the Revolutionary Orientation Committee of the Communist Party Central Committee until his ambassadorial appointment in 1967. Minister of Foreign Relations.

Gil, Elena.
Directress of the Makarenko Pedagogical Institute. Member of the Central Committee of the PCC.

González Marturelos, Luis.
National Coordinator of the Committee for the Defense of the Revolution, 1966-.

Griñán Núñez, Alba.
Ambassador to the United Kingdom, 1965-. Born in 1926. Educated at the University of Oriente and the Sorbonne. Educator. Employed by the Havana Municipal Department of Education. Member of several Cuban delegations to the United Nations. Head of the United Nations Department, Ministry of Foreign Affairs, 1964-1965.

Grobart, Fabio.
Member of the Central Committee of the PCC.

Guevara, Alfredo.
Head of the Cuban Institute of Cinema Arts, a leader in the Federation of University Students (FEU) in the late 1940s.

Guillén, Nicolás.
President of the Union of Writers and Artists of Cuba.

Gusmán, Arturo.
Minister of Mining and Metallurgy, 1967-.

Hart Dávalos, Armando.
Organizing secretary of the Central Committee of the PCC, and member of the Political Bureau. Minister of Education, 1961-1966. An intellectual of middle class background. Married to Haydée Santamaría.

Hernández, Melba.
President of the Cuban Committee of Solidarity with Vietnam, Cambodia and Laos. Participated in the attack on the Moncada Barracks, captured and imprisoned. Leader in the 26th of July Movement throughout the struggle against Batista. Married to Jesús Montane.

Lage, Marcos.
Minister of the Sugar Industry.

Lianusa Gobel, José "Pepe".
Former Minister of Education. Olympic basketball player. Early member of the July 26th Movement. Member of the July 26th Movement Committee in exile responsible for organization in 1958. Very close friend and confidant to Fidel Castro.

López Muiño, Fernando.
Cuban ambassador to Mexico.

Lusson, Enrique.
Minister of Transportation. Member of the Central Committee of the PCC.

Luzardo, Manuel.
Minister of Interior Commerce, 1962-. PSP leader during the Batista regime.

Machado Ventura, José Ramón.
Minister of Public Health, 1961-1968. Member of the Central Committee of the PCC and First Secretary of the Party in Havana Province.

Malmierca, Isidoro.
Director of *Granma,* Cuba's chief newspaper, until 1967. Member of the Secretariat of the Central Committee of the PCC. Deputy Director of the Cuban Fishing Institute.

Marinello, Juan.
Cuban delegate to UNESCO 1963-. Born in 1896. Educated at the Universities of Havana and Madrid. Professor in the Institute of Modern Languages, University of Havana. President of the Popular Socialist Party during the 1940s and 1950s. Rector of the University of Havana, 1962-1963. Author of numerous books and articles.

Martín, Miguel.
Member of the Central Committee of the PCC. Former First Secretary of the Young Communist League (UJC).

Meléndez, Roberto.
Official of the Ministry of Foreign Relations. Member of the Central Committee of the PCC.

Menéndez Tomassevich, Raúl.
Brigade Commander (Major General), Chief of the Eastern Army of the FAR.

Milián, Arnaldo.
First Secretary of the PCC in Las Villas Province and Member of the PCC Central Committee.

Miret Prieto, Pedro.
Vice Minister of the FAR. Chief of the Artillery. Major. Old university friend of Castro. Deputy Prime Minister in charge of the Basic Industry Sector. Minister of Mining, Fuel and Metallurgy. Member of the PCC Secretariat.

Montane Oropesa, Jesús.
Minister of Communications 1963-. University graduate. Major. Former accountant for the Cuban branch of General Motors. Early supporter of Castro. Published an anti-Batista pamphlet before the Moncada attack. Took part in the attack on the Moncada Barracks in 1953. In prison during most of the Batista Regime. Member of the Central Committee of the PCC. Head of the Association of Cuban-Soviet Friendship National Commission established in 1969 to coordinate activities in honor of the centennial of Lenin's birth. Married to Melba Hernández.

Mora Becarra, Alberto.
Cuban politician. Born in 1934. Educated at the University of Havana. Undersecretary of Defense, 1959. Minister of Foreign Trade, 1960-1964.

Naranjo, Pepín.
Member of the PCC Central Committee.

Naranjo Morales, José.
Minister of the Food Industry, 1966-. Member of the Directorio Estudiantil. Minister of Interior, 1959-1961.

Núñez Jiménez, Antonio.
First President of the Cuban-Soviet Friendship Society. President of the Academy of Sciences. Geographer. Captain in the FAR. Currently ambassador to Peru.

Ochoa, Arnaldo.
Brigade Commander (Major General), Chief of the Western Army of the FAR.

Oliva Pérez, Mario.
Head of National Agricultural Development (DAP) and Member of the PCC Central Committee.

Otero Molina, José.
First Deputy Minister of Public Health.

Oza, Enrique de la.
Director of *Bohemia*. Former editor of *Revolución*.

Pavón, Luis.
Director of *Verde Olivo*, the Armed Forces organ. Head of the National Council of Culture.

Pena, Lázaro.
Secretary General of the Cuban Workers Confederation (CTC), 1961-1965. PSP Leader and labor organizer since the 1930s. Member of the Central Committee of the PCC. Elected General Secretary of the CTC in 1973. Died March 11, 1974.

Perada, Roberto.
Director of the Foreign Relations Department of the Ministry of Public Health.

Pérez, Faustino.
President of the National Institute of Water Conservation. With Castro on the GRANMA expedition. Organized the Resistencia Cívica against Batista in 1957. Member of the Central Committee of the PCC. Currently ambassador to Bulgaria.

Pérez Herrero, Antonio.
Member of the Secretariat of the PCC.

Pineiro Losada, Manuel.
Member of the Central Committee of the PCC. Deputy Minister of the Interior.

Polanco, Rafael.
Deputy Head of Foreign Relations of the PCC.

Portuondo, José Antonio.
Director of the Institute of Literature and Linguistics.

Ramírez Cruz, José.
President of ANAP (National Association of Small Farmers). Member of the Central Committee of the PCC.

Risquet, Jorge.

Former Minister of Labor. Member of the Secretariat of the Central Committee of the PCC. Captain in militia.

Roa García, Raúl.

Minister of Foreign Affairs, 1959-. Former professor of the University of Havana. Dean of the Social Sciences, 1948-1959. Cuban representative to the Organization of American States, 1956-1958. Author of numerous books including *Retorno a la alborada.*

Roca, Blas (Francisco Calderío).

President of the Commission for Constitutional Studies of the PCC. Former Secretary-General of the PSP. Member of the Secretariat of the PCC. Thought to be close to Fidel Castro.

Rodríguez, Carlos Rafael..

National Secretary of the Cuban Communist Party, 1966-. Member of the Communist Party since 1932 and its Executive Committee since 1940. Director of the School of Economics, University of Havana, 1960-1962. Editor of *Hoy,* 1959-1962. President of the National Land Reform Institute, 1961-1965. Minister of the Revolutionary Government of Cuba. Minister and Chairman of the Commission for Economic Science. Deputy Prime Minister in charge of the Foreign Sector.

Rodríguez, Rolando.

General Director of the Book Institute (Instituto del Libro).

Rodríguez Rodríguez, Basilio.

Minister of Labor, 1965-1967. Began as a young Fidelista and worked his way up through the ranks. Member of the Central Committee, PCC.

Rojas, Ursinio.

Secretary General of the National Union of Agricultural Workers. PSP leader during the Machado and Batista periods. Member of the Political Bureau and leader among sugar workers.

Ruis, Fabio.

Deputy Director of the National Institute of Sports, Physical Education and Recreation.

Ruiz Bravo, Fernando.

First Commander (Colonel), Head of the Department of Schools and Academies of the Ministry of the FAR.

Sánchez Manduley, Celia.

Minister of the Presidency and the Council of Ministers 1966-. Born in Pilón in the Oriente Province. Daughter of a physician. Joined Castro's movement in 1954. Was not allowed by Castro to go on the GRANMA expedition but joined his forces in the Sierra Maestra shortly thereafter.

Organizer of the July 26th Movement in the cities. Fidel Castro's housekeeper. Felt by some to be Fidel's closest advisor.

Santamaría, Aldo.
Corvette Commander (Rear Admiral), Deputy Minister-Chief of the Cuban Navy. Member of the PCC Central Committee.

Santamaría, Haydée "Yeye".
Director of the Casa de las Américas. Member of the Central Committee of the PCC. Born in Las Villas. One of two women who took part in the attack on the Moncada Barracks, 1953. Imprisoned and tortured. Released in 1954. Veteran of the Sierra Maestra. Active in urban warfare, 1957-1959. Close friend of Fidel Castro. Married to Armando Hart.

Serra, Clementina.
National Directress of Community Day Nurseries. Member of the Central Committee of the PCC.

Soto, Lionel.
President of the Council for the Plan for Technological Training in Soils, Fertilizer and Livestock. University friend of Fidel Castro. Student leader of the Communist Party during the early 1950s. Director of the Schools of Revolutionary Instruction, 1960-1961. Secretary of the Board of Coordination and Inspection of Las Villas Province in 1961.

Torralba González, Diocles.
Major. First Deputy Minister of the FAR, Deputy Prime Minister in charge of the Sugar Industry Sector.

Torres, Armando.
Minister of Justice.

Torres, Felipe.
First Secretary of the Camagüey Provincial Committee of the PCC. Member of the Central Committee of the PCC.

Valdés Menéndez, Ramiro.
Minister of Interior 1961-1969. With Castro in the Sierra Maestra. Major. Police Chief, 1959. Supervised the Committees for the Defense of the Revolution, 1959-1961. Member of the Political Bureau of the Communist Party of Cuba. Deputy Prime Minister in charge of the Construction Sector.

Valdés Vivó, Raúl.
Cuban ambassador to the Democratic Republic of Vietnam, the Provisional Revolutionary Government of the Republic of South Vietnam and the Royal Government of the National Union of Cambodia. Former Secretary-General of the Juventud Socialista, the youth section of the PSP.

Vecino, Fernando.
Brigade Commander (Major General), Deputy Minister in charge of the Political Department of the Ministry of the FAR.

Veiga, Roberto.
General Secretary of the Central Organization of Cuban Trade Unions following death of Lázaro Peña in 1974.

Vera, Ernesto.
President of the Journalists Union of Cuba.

Yabur Maluf, Alfredo.
Former Minister of Justice, President of the Supreme Council on Urban Reform. Member of the Central Committee of the PCC.

Dominican Republic

Compiled by
Richard V. Salisbury
Assistant Professor of History
State University College,
Geneseo, New York

Albuquerque, Félix.
Head of the National Union of Organized Truck Drivers (UNACHOSIN), the labor arm of the Dominican Revolutionary Party.

Amiama Tío, Fernando.
Secretary of Foreign Affairs, 1968-1970. Ambassador to the United Nations, 1971.

Amiama Tío, Luis.
One of the two surviving assassins of Trujillo. Member of the Council of State, 1961-1963. Leader of the Liberal Evolutionary Party. Secretary without Portfolio, 1968-1970.

Aristy, Héctor.
Constitutionalist Minister to the Presidency during the 1965 Civil War. Leader of the Pro Chinese 24 of April Movement. Deported in 1970.

Balaguer, Joaquín.
President (1960-1961, 1966-1970, 1970-1974, 1974-). Born September 1, 1907 in Santiago de los Caballeros. Earned a law degree at the University of Santo Domingo and a Doctorate of Law at the Sorbonne. Professor of Law and Diplomat. Served in Madrid, 1932-1935. Under-Secretary of Foreign Affairs, 1936-1940. Minister to Colombia, 1940-1946. Alternate Representative to the United Nations, 1947. Secretary of Foreign Affairs, 1954-1955. Secretary of Education and Arts, 1955-1957. Vice-President, 1957-1960. Founder of the Reformista Party, 1962. Voluntary exile in the United States, 1962-1965.

Bautista de Suárez, Altagracia.
Secretary of Education and Arts, 1970-1972. Secretary of Industry and Commerce, 1973.

Beauchamps Javier, Juan René.
Secretary of Interior, 1971. Secretary without Portfolio, 1971. Inspector General of the Army, 1971.

Benoit, Pedro Bartolomé.
Air Force Colonel. President of San Isidro Military Junta April 27 to May 7, 1965. Member of Imbert's "Government of National Reconstruction" May 7 to August 30, 1965.

Bonnelly, Rafael F.
Conservative politician and lawyer. Born 1905. Deputy to the National Assembly, 1939-1941. Deputy to the Senate, 1941. Secretary of Interior and Police, 1941-1942. Law Professor at Ciudad Trujillo University, 1942-1946. Secretary of Labor, 1946. Founder of the National Civic Union, 1961. President of the Council of State, 1961-1963. Presidential candidate of the National Integration Movement in 1966.

Bosch, Juan.
Dominican intellectual and political leader. Born June 30, 1909. In exile in Cuba, Puerto Rico, Costa Rica, Venezuela, and the United States, 1937-1961. Founder of the Dominican Revolutionary Party, 1939. President of the Dominican Revolutionary Party, 1939-1966. Member of the Cayo Confites Expedition, 1947. Returned from exile in 1961 to campaign for the presidency. Elected President on December 20, 1962. Inaugurated on February 27, 1963. Deposed by a right wing civil-military coup on September 25, 1963. In exile in Puerto Rico, 1963-1965. Unsuccessful Dominican Revolutionary Party candidate for the presidency in 1966. Exile in Spain and France, 1967-1970. Resigns from the Dominican Revolutionary Party in November of 1973 and forms the Dominican Liberation Party.

Brache Lora, José Antonio.
Secretary of Labor, 1971. Secretary of Industry and Commerce, 1972.

Brea Peña, José Antonio.
Secretary of Industry and Commerce, 1970. Owner of Radio Commercial.

Caamaño Grullón, Claudio.
Half-brother of the late Colonel Francisco Caamaño Deñó. Member of the Constitutionalist Military Command during the 1965 Civil War. Participant in the February, 1973 guerrilla invasion of the Dominican Republic. Currently in exile.

Casimiro Castro, Pablo Rafael.
Senator. Expelled from the Dominican Revolutionary Party in April, 1973.

Dominici, Porfirio.
Ambassador and Permanent Representative to the United Nations, 1972.

Fernández, Jaime Manuel.
Presidential candidate of the National Conciliation Movement in 1970. Secretary of Foreign Affairs, 1970-1972. Secretary of Labor, 1972.

Fiallo, Viriato A.
Physician and civic leader. Presidential candidate of the National Civic Union in 1962.

Fiallo Cáceres, Fabio.
Judge. Appointed Attorney-General in May, 1973.

Genao Espaillat, Luis.
Former guerrilla commander of the 14 of June Movement. Deputy Secretary of Police and Interior, 1971.

Gil, Secundino.
President of the Dominican Revolutionary Party, 1974.

Goico Morales, Carlos Rafael.
Vice-President, 1970-1974.

Gómez Berges, Víctor.
Secretary of Education and Arts, 1970-1972. Secretary of Foreign Affairs, 1972-1974. Director of the National Youth Movement.

Guerrero Aula, Jaime.
Secretary of Labor, 1973.

Guzmán Fernández, Silvestre Antonio.
Hacendado and political leader. Secretary of Agriculture under Bosch in 1963. Proposed for Provisional President during the 1965 Civil War. Presidential candidate for the Dominican Revolutionary Party in 1966. Presidential candidate in 1974 endorsed by the parties (Dominican Revolutionary Party, Quisqueyano Democratic Party, Social Christian Revolutionary Party, National Civic Union, and the Dominican Popular Movement) which joined together in the "Santiago Agreement." Candidacy withdrawn just prior to the May, 1974 election.

Imbert Barrera, Antonio.
One of the two surviving assassins of Trujillo. Brigadier General in the Dominican Armed Forces. Member of the Council of State, 1962-1963. Member of the anti-Bosch civil-military faction in 1963. President of the

"Government of National Reconstruction," May 7 to August 30, 1965. Inspector-General of the Armed Forces, 1973.

Isa Conde, Narciso.
Secretary-General of the Dominican Communist Party.

Jiménez Grullón, Juan Isidro.
Writer and politician. Member of the Cayo Confites Expedition, 1947. Breaks with the National Civic Union in 1962 to form the Social Democratic Alliance Party. Presidential candidate of the Social Democratic Alliance Party in 1962 and 1970.

Jiménez Rodríguez, Manuel.
Former Mayor of Santo Domingo. Allegedly involved in an anti-Balaguer plot in 1972. Currently in exile.

Kasse Acta, Rafael.
Elected Rector of the University of Santo Domingo in 1970. Professor of Dentistry. Member of the Dominican Revolutionary Party.

Lajara Burgos, Luis Homero.
Retired Rear-Admiral. Presidential candidate in 1974 for the Democratic Popular Party.

Llueberes Montas, Salvador.
Air Force Commander. Secretary of Interior and Police, 1971.

López Molina, Máximo.
Leader of the Pro Castro Dominican Popular Movement. Currently in exile.

Lora, Francisco Augusto.
Vice-President, 1966-1970. Resigns from the Reformista Party to join the Democratic Integration Action Movement. Presidential candidate in 1970 for the Democratic Integration Action Movement.

Martínez Francisco, Antonio.
Wealthy businessman. Secretary-General of the Dominican Revolutionary Party, 1965. Secretary of Finance, 1970.

Miolán, Ángel.
Dominican Revolutionary Party leader. Labor adviser to Bosch, 1963. Secretary without Portfolio, 1971. Director of Tourism, 1971.

Moreno Martínez, Alfonso.
Presidential candidate of the Social Christian Party in 1962. Presidential candidate for the Social Christian Revolutionary Party in 1970.

Nivar Seijas, Rafael Neit.
Dominican military leader. Member of the Civil-Military Junta,

January 16-18, 1962. Head of the First Army Brigade, 1971. Chief of Police, 1971. Secretary to the President, 1973. Promoted to Major-General, 1973.

Ornes, Horacio Julio.
  Dominican "Establishment" figure. Member of Cayo Confites Expedition, 1947. Presidential candidate of the Vanguardia Party in 1962. Ambassador and Permanent Representative to the United Nations, 1970.

Peña Gómez, José Francisco.
  Secretary-General of the Dominican Revolutionary Party, 1966-1973. Youth leader of the Dominican Revolutionary Party in 1962. Important leader of the rebels in the 1965 Civil War. Emerged as the Dominican Revolutionary Party's maximum leader in the wake of Juan Bosch's split from the party ranks in December, 1973.

Perdono Robles, Tácito.
  Leader of the Dominican Popular Movement.

Pérez y Pérez, Enrique.
  Dominican military leader. Chief of Staff, 1970. Secretary of Defense, 1970. Secretary of Interior and Police, 1970. Head of the First Army Brigade, 1971. Commander in Chief of the Army, 1973. One of two Major-Generals in the Dominican Armed Forces. Rival of General Nivar Seijas.

Reid Cabral, Donald Joseph.
  Businessman and political leader. Born June 9, 1923. Educated at the University of Santo Domingo. President of the Automobile Dealer's Association, 1949-1962. Vice-President of the Council of State, 1962-1963. Secretary of Foreign Affairs, September to December, 1963. President of the 1963-1965 Triumvirate.

Ruiz Tejada, Manuel Ramón.
  President of the Supreme Court. Interim President, 1970.

Salvador Ortiz, S.
  Ambassador to the United States, 1970.

Sandino de Jesús, César.
  Secretary of Agriculture, 1971.

Selimen, Carlos.
  Businessman. Secretary of Finance, 1973.

Taveras Guzmán, Juan Arístides.
  Attorney-General, 1973.

Uribe Silva, Adriano.
  President of the Senate.

Vidal Martínez, Rafael.
  Secretary of Labor, 1972.

Volman, Sacha.
  Rumanian born immigrant. Early organizer of the Dominican Revolutionary Party. Adviser to President Bosch. Founded the Inter-American Center for Social Studies in 1962. Labor adviser to the Falconbridge Nickel Mines, 1971.

Wessin y Wessin, Elías.
  Dominican military and political leader. Son of a Lebanese trader. Member of the civil-military group that overthrew President Bosch in September, 1963. Major leader of the Loyalist forces in the 1965 Civil War. Presidential candidate of the Quisqueyano Democratic Party in 1970. Exiled to Spain in 1971 for plotting against President Balaguer. Vice-Presidential candidate in 1974 for the "Santiago Agreement" coalition. Still in exile.

Ecuador

Compiled by
Jorge H. Valdivieso
Professor of Spanish
American Graduate School of
International Management

Acosta Velasco, Jorge.
  Lawyer. Former Congressman, Minister of the Treasury, Minister of Defense, and Ambassador to Spain. He is a member of a family of bankers (Banco del Pichincha) and leaders of the Conservative Party (Partido Conservador Ecuatoriano).

Almeida Játiva, Marco.
  Retired General. Minister of Defense from January, 1973 to the present in the military government of General Rodríguez Lara.

Aguayo Cubillo, Pedro.
  Civil Engineer. Chairman of the Board of Economic Planning and Coordination (Junta Nacional de Planificación y Coordinación Económica) from February, 1972 to the present.

Aguirre Azanza, Carlos.
  Colonel (Army). Secretary General of the Administration from February, 1972 to the present in the military government of General Rodríguez Lara.

Aroca, José.
  Labor leader. General Secretary of the Ecuadorian Confederation of Catholic Workers (Confederación Ecuatoriana de Obreros Católicos).

Arosemena Gómez, Otto.

Lawyer. Former Congressman and Senator from the province of Guayas. In November 1967, a constitutional assembly elected him as Provisional President of the Republic. He criticized the United States at Punta del Este, Uruguay, and refused to sign the Declaration of Presidents of the Americas.

Arosemena Monroy, Carlos Julio.

Lawyer. Former Congressman, Minister of Defense, and Chairman of the House of Representatives (Cámara de Diputados). Elected Vice-President of the Republic in 1960, he replaced Velasco Ibarra in the presidency in November 1961. He was overthrown by the military in July 1963.

Baquerizo Maldonado, José.

University Professor. President of the Catholic University of Guayaquil.

Benítez Vinueza, Leopoldo.

Career diplomat. Ambassador to the United Nations. He was elected President of the General Assembly for the period 1973-74.

Bucaram, Asaad.

Businessman. Director of C.F.P. Party (Concentración de Fuerzas Populares). Former Mayor of Guayaquil, Congressman, and Councilman. In 1973, he was nominated as presidential candidate by C.F.P., but the military coup-d'état of 1973 prevented the country from having elections.

Cordero, Gregorio.

University Professor. President of the University of Cuenca.

Córdova Galarza, Gonzalo.

Lawyer. General Superintendent of the Banking System from April 1974 to the present.

Durán Arcentales, Luis Guillermo.

Colonel (Army). Minister of Education from June, 1973 to the present.

Durán Ballén, Sixto.

Architect. Mayor of Quito from June, 1970 to the present. Former Minister of Public Works in the cabinet of Camilo Ponce (1956), and Senator chosen by the educational private institutions.

Durán Díaz, Edmundo.

University Professor. President of the University of Guayaquil.

Echeverría, Bernardino.

Archbishop of Guayaquil. Member of the Franciscan Order. Chancellor of the Catholic University of Guayaquil.

Erazo, Ernesto.
University student. President of the Federation of University Students (FEUE: Federación de Estudiantes Universitarios del Ecuador).

Espinosa, Germánico.
Economist. General Manager of the Central Bank of Ecuador from October, 1973 to the present.

Espinosa, Solón.
Colonel. General Comptroller of the Nation from October, 1972 to the present.

Gallo, Gonzalo.
Lawyer. Attorney General (Fiscal General de la República).

Herrera, Marco.
Economist. Director of the Institute of Agrarian Reform (IERAC: Instituto Ecuatoriano de Reforma Agraria y Colonización).

Huerta Montalvo, Francisco.
Lawyer. Director of the Liberal Party (Partido Liberal Radical). Because he objected to the policies of the military government, was exiled in the Amazon jungle for almost one year. He remains a powerful figure in the opposition.

Jarrín Ampudia, Gustavo.
Captain (Navy). Minister of Natural Resources from February, 1972 to the present.

Karolys, Gonzalo.
Lawyer. Procurator-General of the Nation from March, 1972 to the present. He was a strong student leader at the university, and a very active member of the Socialist party.

Leguísamo, Mario.
Teacher. President of the National Union of Educators (UNE: Unión Nacional de Educadores). He was the leader of the opposition against the Minister of Education, Colonel Luis Guillermo Durán Arcentales.

Leoro Franco, Galo.
Lawyer. Ambassador to the Organization of American States from March, 1972 to the present.

Maldonado Lince, Guillermo.
Lawyer. Minister of Agriculture from February, 1973 to the present.

Maldonado Mejía, Raúl.
Doctor of Medicine. Minister of Health from February, 1972 to the present.

Malo, Hernán.
Jesuit. President of the Catholic University of Quito.

Moncayo, Jaime.
Economist. Minister of Finance from January, 1974 to the present.

Morejón, Luis.
General (Army). Minister of Labor and Welfare from February, 1972 to the present.

Muñoz Vega, Pablo.
Cardinal-Archbishop of Quito. Former Provincial of the order in Ecuador and Professor of Philosophy in Rome.

Oleas Zambrano, Gonzalo.
Lawyer. General Secretary of the Socialist Party. University Professor. Former member of the Congress.

Orellana, Rubén.
Engineer. University Professor. President of the National Polytechnical Institute. Former Senator.

Ortega Jaramillo, Rubén.
Lawyer. Writer. Mayor of Loja from June, 1970 to the present.

Ortiz, Benjamín.
Journalist. President of the National Union of Journalists (UNP: Unión Nacional de Periodistas).

Paredes, Antonio José Lucio.
Lawyer. Career diplomat. Minister of Foreign Affairs from February, 1972 to the present.

Pazmiño, Estuardo.
University Professor. Acting President of the Central University of Quito.

Péndola, Juan.
Architect. Mayor of Guayaquil from 1970 to the present.

Plaza Lasso, Galo.
Agriculturalist. President of the Republic from 1948 to 1952, his was the first completed term in the office of the presidency of Ecuador in twenty-eight years. Took office in May, 1968 as Secretary General of the Organization of American States. Former Minister of Defense.

Ponce Enríquez, Camilo.
Lawyer. President of the Republic from 1956 to 1960. Minister of the Interior in the fourth presidency of Velasco Ibarra. Founder of the Social Christian Party (Partido Social Cristiano).

Poveda, Alfredo.
Rear Admiral (Navy). Minister of the Interior from June, 1973 to the present.

Quevedo Toro, Alberto.
Lawyer and Economist. Ambassador to the United States from August, 1972 to the present. Former Minister of Finance and university professor, he studied in Ecuador and the United States.

Rodríguez Lara, Guillermo.
General of the Republic (Army). President of the Republic from February 15, 1972 to the present. He was chosen as head of the government by the military leaders who forced President Velasco Ibarra to resign.

Rodríguez Palacio, Rafael.
Colonel (Corps of Engineers). Minister of Public Works from February, 1972 to the present.

Rosales Ramos, Francisco.
Economist. Minister of Industry and Trade from February, 1973 to the present.

Serrano Aguilar, Alejandro.
Lawyer. College Professor. Mayor of Cuenca from June, 1970 to the present.

Trujillo, Julio César.
Lawyer. Director of the Conservative Party (Partido Conservador Ecuatoriano). Former President of the Federation of Catholic University Students (JUC: Juventud Universitaria Católica).

Valdivieso Alba, Tomás.
Lawyer. President of the Supreme Court of Justice of Ecuador.

Valdivieso Eguiguren, Rogelio.
Lawyer. University Professor. Former member of Congress. He was the only member of the Conservative Party in Velasco's cabinet of 1968, serving as Minister of Foreign Affairs. Former Ambassador to Bolivia and Portugal.

Veintimilla, Federico.
Lawyer. Director of ARNE Party (Acción Revolucionaria Nacional Ecuatoriana).

Velasco Ibarra, José María.
Lawyer. University Professor. President of the Republic five times — 1933, 1943, 1952, 1960, 1968 — he was overthrown four times, com-

pleting only one term. He lives in voluntary exile in Argentina where he teaches international law.

Vivar, José María.
Lawyer. University Professor. President of the University of Loja.

El Salvador

Compiled by
Kenneth J. Grieb, Associated Professor of History and Coordinator of Latin American Studies, Wisconsin State University – Oshkosh

Astacio López, Julio Ernesto.
Minister of Public Health and Social Assistance of the Republic of El Salvador, commencing in 1972. Born March 12, 1932 in San Salvador. Doctor of Medicine from the National University of El Salvador, 1960. Post-graduate study at the University of Pennsylvania, Walter Reed General Hospital in Washington, D.C., and the Universities of Munich and Erlangen, in West Germany. Author of various medical studies published in El Salvador. Member of the various Salvadoran medical associations.

Borgonovo Pohl, Maurico Alfredo.
Minister of Foreign Relations of the Republic of El Salvador, commencing in 1972. Born December 20, 1939 in San Salvador. Mechanical Engineering Degree from the Massachusetts Institute of Technology. Director General of Foreign Policy in the Ministry of Foreign Relations, 1972. President of the Salvadoran Association of Industries, 1966-1972.

Chávez, Rogelio Alfredo.
Minister of Labor and Social Planning of the Republic of El Salvador, commencing in 1972. Born May 20, 1924. Doctor of Jurisprudence and Social Sciences from the National University of El Salvador. Law Professor at the National University of El Salvador. Has held various positions with the Ministry of Labor and Social Work, the Salvadoran Social Security Institute, the Tribunal of Justice, and the Agricultural Bank of El Salvador.

Gavidia Hidalgo, Vicente Amado.
Minister of the Treasury of the Republic of El Salvador commencing in 1970. Born September 13, 1919 in Guadalupe, San Vicente. Doctorate in Economic Sciences from the National University of El Salvador, 1956. M.A. in Economics from the University of Kansas. Director of the Department of Economic Investigations of the Central Reserve Bank of

El Salvador, Technical Consultant to the Departments of Financial Administration of Venezuela, Chile, and Nicaragua. Sub-Secretary of the Treasury. Member of the Board of Directors of the Salvadoran Social Security Institute and the Salvadoran Institute of Development and Production, now the Institute of Industrial Development (INCAFI). Professor of Economic Theory and Public Finance in the Faculty of Economics of the National University of El Salvador. Appointed Minister of the Treasury by President Fidel Sánchez Hernández in 1970, and continued in the same position by President Colonel Arturo Armando Molina.

Hidalgo Quehl, Guillermo.

Minister of Economy of the Republic of El Salvador commencing in 1973. Born December 22, 1923 in San Salvador. Doctor of Jurisprudence and Social Sciences from the National University of El Salvador, 1952. Professor of Mercantile and Commercial Law at the National University of El Salvador, 1959-1960. Justice of the Peace in San Salvador. Criminal Justice in Sonsonate and San Salvador. Member of the Legal Staff of the Ministry of Justice, and of the commission which revised the Commercial Code of El Salvador, 1958-1959. Sub-Secretary of the Treasury, 1961. Vice-President of the Central Bank of Reserve of Salvador, 1961-1973.

Llach Hill, Roberto.

Minister of Agriculture and Dairying of the Republic of El Salvador commencing in 1973. Born September 18, 1940 in San Salvador. Bachelor's Degree in Architecture from the University of Pennsylvania. Post-graduate studies at Columbia University. Director of the Central American Institute of Administration of Industries (INCAE). Director of the Salvadoran Coffee Company, 1971. President of the Salvadoran Coffee Company, 1971-1973. Director of the National Department of Coffee, 1971-1973.

Martínez Varela, Juan Antonio.

Minister of the Interior of the Republic of El Salvador, commencing in 1972. Born August 29, 1923 in San Juan Talpa, La Paz. A career military officer, and graduate of the Salvadoran Military Academy. Additional studies at the School of Infantry, Fort Benning, Georgia, and the War College of the Italian Army in Civitavecchia, Rome. Has held numerous command positions within the Army, including service on the General Staff. Military Attaché of Salvadoran Embassies in Guatemala and Honduras. Salvadoran Delegate to the Permanent Commission of the Central American Defense Council. Sub-Director of the Dr. Manuel Enrique Araujo Military Command School. Chief of the Department of Military Justice of the Ministry of Defense. Commander of the Department of Usulután. Presently holds the rank of Colonel. Private Secretary to the President of El Salvador, General Fidel Sánchez Hernández, 1971-1972.

Mayorga Rivas, Enrique.

Vice President of the Republic of El Salvador for the term 1972-1977, and Minister of the Presidency commencing in 1973. Born November 1, 1926 in San Salvador. Pursued legal studies at the Universities of Salamanca, Barcelona and Madrid, Spain. Licenciado in Law, University of Madrid, 1956. Doctor of Jurisprudence and Social Sciences, University of El Salvador, 1958. An active journalist who has written for most of the major newspapers of San Salvador, and particularly as a regular editorial page columnist in *La Prensa Gráfica* and the *Diario Latino*. Chief of the Legal Department of the Banco Capitalzador, 1958-1967. Professor of Journalism History in the Faculty of Humanities and examiner in the Faculties of International, Private, and Business Law, in the Faculty of Jurisprudence and Social Sciences, National University of El Salvador. Secretary General of the Salvadoran Institute of Hispanic Culture. Member of the Supreme Council of the Salvadoran Red Cross, 1962-1963. Secretary General to the President of El Salvador, General Fidel Sánchez Hernández, 1967-1971. First Designate to the Presidency of the Republic, 1970-1972. Elected Vice President of the Republic for the period 1972-1977. Continued as Secretary General to the Presidency, 1972-1973. Minister of the Presidency commencing in 1973.

Molina, Arturo Armando.

President of the Republic of El Salvador for the term 1972-1977. Born August 6, 1927 in San Salvador. A career military officer, who graduated from the Salvadoran Military Academy in 1949. Additional studies in Superior War College of Mexico and the School of Applied Infantry Tactics in Spain. Has held numerous positions in the Armed Forces, serving as the Commander of the Department of Santa Ana, and on the Salvadoran General Staff. Professor of Tactics, Military History, and Strategy in the Escuela Militar Capitán General Barrios, the Escuela Militar General Manuel José Arce, and the Dr. Manuel Enrique Araujo Command School. Has represented Salvador at numerous Inter-American Military Conferences. Presently holds the rank of Colonel. Member of the Board of Directors of the National Railroads of Salvador. Private Secretary to the President of El Salvador, General Fidel Sánchez Hernández, 1969-1971.

Pineda Rodríguez, Rodrigo Raymundo.

Private Secretary to the President of the Republic of El Salvador, Colonel Arturo Armando Molina, commencing in 1972. Born June 8, 1922 in Uluazapa, San Miguel. Doctorate in Jurisprudence and Social Sciences from the National University of El Salvador, 1953. Post graduate study in the Friedrich Wilhems University in Bonn, and the University of Köln, Germany. Professor of Criminology and Examiner in the Faculty of Law of the National University of El Salvador. Justice of the Peace in the Municipality of San Vicente, 1953-1955. Director General of Penal Institutions, Ministry of Justice 1957-1960. Sub-Secretary of Justice, 1960-1961.

Rodríguez, Rubén Alfonso.

President of the Legislative Assembly of the Republic of El Salvador, commencing in 1972. Born October 7, 1922 in Juayuá Sonsonate. Licenciado in Law from the National University of El Salvador, 1956. Director and President, Banco Hipotecario. Director of the National Department of Coffee. Justice of the Peace. Deputy in the National Congress, 1950-1952, and 1970-1974. Alderman of the Municipal Council of Sonsonate. Director of the National Association of Dairymen. Director of the National Coffee Association.

Romero Mena, Carlos Humberto.

Minister of Defense and Public Security of the Republic of El Salvador, commencing in 1972. Born February 29, 1924 in Chalatenango. A career military officer and a graduate of the Salvadoran Military Academy. Has held various command positions within the Army including Director of the Personnel Department of the General Staff, and Chief of the Office of General Command of the Armed Forces. Presently holds the rank of Colonel.

Sánchez, Rogelio.

Minister of Education of the Republic of El Salvador, commencing in 1972. Born January 2, 1932 in San Francisco, Morazán. Doctor of Jurisprudence and Social Sciences from the University of El Salvador. Post graduate studies at the University of Puerto Rico and the Central American Institute of Business and Administration in Managua, Nicaragua. During his student days served as Vice-President of the University Students Association, and President of the Association of Law Students. Professor of Law at the Superior Normal School. Secretary and Director of the Department of Student Well-Being of the National University of El Salvador. Professor of Law at the National University of El Salvador. Deputy and Vice-President of the Legislative Assembly of El Salvador, 1970-1972.

Sánchez Hernández, Fidel.

President of the Republic of El Salvador, 1967-1972. Born July 7, 1917 in El Divisadero, Morazán. Graduate of the Salvadoran Military Academy, 1938, School of Armor, Fort Knox, and the General Staff College of Madrid, Spain, 1954. Career Army Officer, presently holding the rank of General. Salvadoran Military Attaché in Paris, 1954. Salvadoran Delegate to the United Nations Commission in Korea. Commandant of the Department of San Miguel, and Chief of the Thirteenth Infantry Regiment, 1958-1960. Military and Air Attaché at the Salvadoran Embassy in Washington, 1960. Chief of the Salvadoran Delegation to the Inter-American Defense Council 1960-1961. Vice President and Interim President of the Inter-American Defense Council. Inspector General of the Salvadoran Armed Forces. Chief of Staff of the Salvadoran Armed Forces. Minister of Interior, 1962-1966. Second Designate to the Presidency, 1964-1966.

Seaman, Jorge Antonio.

Minister of Public Works of the Republic of El Salvador, commencing in 1972. Born August 30, 1930 in San Salvador. Civil Engineering Degree from the National University of El Salvador, 1953. Post graduate study at the National Autonomous University of Mexico. Chief of the Department of Urbanism of the Salvadoran General Office of Urbanism and Architecture, 1954-1957. Professor in the Faculty of Engineering and Architecture of the National University of El Salvador, 1954-1959. Experience in several private businesses during the 1950s and 60s. Member of the various Salvadoran Engineering Societies, and has held offices in many of them. President of the Chamber of the Salvadoran Construction Industry, 1965-1968. Vice-President of the Inter-American Federation of Construction Industries, 1969-1970.

Silva, José Enrique.

Minister of Justice of the Republic of El Salvador, commencing in 1972. Born April 8, 1930 in Ahuachapán. Doctorate in Jurisprudence and Social Sciences, National University of El Salvador, 1959. During his student career he served as editor of the student journal *Ciencias jurídicas y sociales,* Secretary General of the University Students Association, 1954, and President of the Law Students Association, 1955. Professor of Penal Law and Politics and Vice Dean of the Faculty of Jurisprudence and Social Sciences, National University of El Salvador. Professor on the Faculty of Humanities of the Salvadoran Superior Normal School. Editor of the Journal *La universidad* and *Revista de derecho.* President of the Center of Judicial Studies, and author of numerous publications on Penal and Judicial matters. A member of the Legal Department of the Agricultural and Commercial Bank of El Salvador. Served as Justice of the Peace, Director General of Penal Centers, and as a Member of the Commission which revised the Penal Code of El Salvador. Has represented El Salvador at numerous International Legal Conferences.

Velarde F., Aníbal.

Private Secretary to the President of the Republic of El Salvador, Colonel Arturo Armando Molina, commencing in 1972. Born June 7, 1928 in San Salvador. Now a Colonel, Velarde is a career military officer who has held various command positions. Professor of Logistics and Organization at the Dr. Manuel Enrique Araujo Command School.

Guatemala

Compiled by
Kenneth J. Grieb, Associate
Professor of History
Coordinator of Latin American
Studies, Wisconsin State
University – Oshkosh

Anzueto Vielmann, Gustavo.

Minister of Communications and Public Works of the Republic of Guatemala, 1970-1974. Born March 3, 1930 in Guatemala City. Studies at the University of Texas at Austin and the University of San Carlos. Degree in Architecture from the University of San Carlos. Professor of Architecture at the University of San Carlos. Founder, Secretary, and President of the Association of Guatemalan Architects. Member of the Board of Directors of GUATEL.

Arana Osorio, Carlos Manuel.

President of the Republic of Guatemala for the term 1970-1974. Elected in 1970 as the candidate of the Guatemalan National Liberation Party (MLN) and the Institutional Democratic Party (PID). Born July 17, 1918 in Barberena, Santa Rosa. A career military officer, and a graduate of the Guatemalan Polytechnic Institute (The National Military Academy) in 1939. Reached the rank of Colonel in 1935, and currently holds the rank of General of Brigade to which he was promoted in 1971. Director of Roads in various provinces during the period 1939-1945. Engineer in the construction of Roosevelt Highway, 1945-1946. Professor of Spanish and Geography at the Polytechnic Institute, 1946-1948. Secretary to the Commander of the Armed Forces, 1949-1951. Held various military commands, including Commandant of the First Infantry Regiment of the Presidential Guard, 1954. Director of the Polytechnic Institute 1954-1957. Sub-Secretary of National Defense, 1957-1958. Military Attaché of the Guatemalan Embassy to the United States, and Guatemalan Delegate to the Inter-American Defense Council, 1958-1959 and 1965-1966. Commander of the military zone of Jutiapa, 1963-1965, and of the military zone of Zacapa, 1966-1968. Guatemalan Ambassador in Nicaragua, 1968-1969, at which time he resigned to enter the Presidential campaign.

Arenales Catalán, Jorge.

Minister of Foreign Relations of the Republic of Guatemala, 1970-1974. Born April 19, 1914 in Guatemala City. Licenciado in Law from the National University of San Carlos. Additional studies in international law at the American University, Washington D.C. Sub-Secretary of Agriculture and Mining, 1944. Guatemalan Consul in New York, 1945. Minister of Economy and Public Works, 1954-1956.

Cáceres Lehnhoff, Eduardo.
Vice-President of the Republic of Guatemala 1970-1974. Born June 2, 1906 in Guatemala City. Licenciado in Law from the National University in Guatemala, 1930. Sub-Secretary of the Ministry of Development, 1944-1945. Deputy in the National Congress of Guatemala, 1949-1953 and 1962-1963. Deputy in the National Constituent Assembly of Guatemala, 1954-1956. Has attended numerous international conferences particularly relating to law. Member of the Guatemalan Association of Lawyers, serving as President 1960-1961. Member of the Guatemalan Rotary Club, having served as its President and Governor of the Rotary Club district for Central America. Hobby is traveling and has visited 63 countries.

Fuentes Mohr, Alberto.
Minister of Foreign Relations of the Republic of Guatemala, 1968-1970. Born November 22, 1927. Doctorate in Political and Economic Sciences from the London School of Economics. Employee of the Department of Trusteeship Administration of the United Nations, 1956-1957. Chief of the Foreign Commerce Section of the Mexican Office of the Economic Commission for Latin America, 1957-1958. Secretary General and Permanent Secretary of the General Treaty of the Inter-American Economic Integration. 1961-1962. Chief of the Joint Mission of Economic Planning for Central America, 1962-1966. Representative of the Central American Common Market to the European Economic Community, 1965. Guatemalan Member of the Board of Directors of the Central American Bank of Economic Integration, 1968-1969. Central American Representative to the Inter-American Committee of the Alliance for Progress, 1968-1969. Guatemalan Member of the Board of Governors of the International Bank of Reconstruction and Development, and Inter-American Development Bank, and the International Monetary Fund, 1966-1968. Minister of the Treasury and Public Credit, 1966-1968.

Fuentes Pieruccini, Mario.
Presidential candidate of the Revolutionary Party (PR) in the 1970 election. Born October 7, 1921 in Quezaltenango. Law Degree from the University of San Carlos. Professor of International Law at the University of San Carlos. Auditor of the Guatemalan Central Bank. Guatemalan Ambassador to the San Salvador Conference of 1950, which founded ODECA. Deputy in the Guatemalan National Assembly, 1949-1951. Second Vice President of the National Assembly. President of the National Assembly, 1966-1967. Minister of the Treasury and Public Credit, 1966-1969.

Herrera Ibarguen, Roberto.
Minister of Government of the Republic of Guatemala, 1970-1974. Born October 11, 1921 in Guatemala City. B.A. Degree from Dartmouth College, 1943, M.A. and Ph.D. degrees from Columbia University in

International Law. Service in the Judicial Department of the Secretary General of the United Nations, 1947-1952. Guatemalan Ambassador to El Salvador, 1954-1956. Guatemalan Ambassador to Panama. Deputy in the Guatemalan National Congress, 1964-1970. Member of the National Liberation Movement (MLN) and President of its Political Council, 1968 to the present. Member of the Permanent Court of Arbitration at the Hague, 1967 to present. Director of the Bank of Agronomy. Has served as Guatemalan delegate to various international Judicial Congresses. Guatemalan delegate to the Second Extraordinary Inter-American Conference in Rio de Janiero, 1965. Member of the Guatemalan delegation to the United Nations General Assembly, 1967-1968. Member of the Guatemalan delegation to the First Extraordinary Assembly of the Organization of American States, Washington, 1970.

Lamport Rodil, Jorge.

Minister of Finance of the Republic of Guatemala, 1970-1974. Born January 3, 1928 in Guatemala City. Studied at the University of British Columbia and the University of San Carlos. Engaged in private business throughout most of career. Professor at the Rafael Landivar University, 1967 to present. Deputy in the National Congress of Guatemala, 1966-1970.

Laugerud García, Kjell Eugenio.

President of the Republic of Guatemala for the term 1974-. Elected in the 1974 election as the candidate of the National Liberation Party (MLN) and the Institutional Democratic Party (PID). Born January 24, 1930 in Guatemala City. A career military officer who graduated from the Guatemalan Polytechnic Institute (the National Military Academy), in 1949. Served as a Professor and Chief of Studies at the Polytechnic Institute at various times throughout his career. Director of the Polytechnic Institue, 1965-1966. Assistant Chief of Staff and Inspector General of the Guatemalan Army, 1966-1967. Guatemalan Military Attaché to the United States and Chief of the Guatemalan Delegation to the Inter-American Defense Council. Chief of the Staff of the Guatemalan Army, 1970-1972. Minister of Defense, 1972-1973, a post from which he resigned in January of 1973 to become a candidate for the Presidency. Presently holds the rank of Brigadier General.

López Rivera, Lionel Fernando.

Minister of Social Work and Social Planning of the Republic of Guatemala, 1970-1974. Born April 29, 1928 in Guatemala City. Licenciado in Social and Juridical Sciences. Deputy in and Secretary of the National Constituent Assembly of Guatemala, 1964-1965. Deputy in the National Congress of Guatemala, 1966-1970. President and Vice President of the Political Council of the Institutional Democratic Party (PID).

Maldonado Aguirre, Aledandro.
   Minister of Education of the Republic of Guatemala, 1970-1974. Born January 6, 1936 in Guatemala City. Bachelor's Degree in Elementary Education from the Instituto Modelo. Licenciado in Juridical and Social Sciences from the University of San Carlos. Professor of Sociology at the Rafael Landivar University. Deputy in the Congress of Guatemala. Author of various legal studies and articles in various Guatemalan newspapers. Director of Social Politics of the National Liberation Movement (MLN).

Marroquín Rojas, Clemente.
   Founder and Editor of the newspaper *La Hora,* inaugurated in 1920, and continuing to the present. Born August 12, 1897 in Valle de Jumay. Law Degree from the University of San Carlos. Also Law studies at the University of Honduras. .Has written for most of the newspapers in Guatemala since 1920. During a period in exile from 1931 to 1944, his articles appeared in various newspapers throughout Central America and Mexico. Guatemalan Consul in Barcelona, Spain, 1926. Deputy in the Guatemalan National Constituent Assembly, 1927. Director General of Roads, 1927. Deputy in the National Constituent Assembly, 1945. Minister of Economics, 1946-1947. Deputy of the National Congress, 1952-1959. Vice-President of the Republic of Guatemala and President of the Guatemalan Council of State, 1966-1970. Author of numerous historical and political studies, and of countless articles and editorials that have appeared in journals and newspapers in Guatemala.

Martínez Gutiérrez, Mario Adolfo.
   Minister of Agriculture of the Republic of Guatemala, 1970-1974. Born April 30, 1936. Diploma in Agricultural Engineering, University of San Carlos, 1960. Previous studies at the University of San Carlos, and in Mexico and in Brazil. Has held numerous posts within the Ministry of Agriculture including Director of the Department of Agricultural Investigations and Chief of Experimental Stations, 1965-1970. Professor of Statistics and Hydrology of the Faculty of Agronomy of the University of San Carlos, 1965 to the present. Vice Dean of the Directive Council of the Faculty of Agronomy, University of San Carlos, 1965-1969. Author of numerous publications dealing with various facets of agriculture.

Méndez Montenegro, Julio César.
   President of the Republic of Guatemala, 1966-1970. Born November 23, 1915, in Guatemala City. Law Degree from the University of San Carlos. Post graduate study at the University of Santiago, Chile. President of the Student Law Association of Guatemala. President of the Popular Liberating Front during the revolution of 1944, and an active participant in the revolutions of July and October of that year. Professor of the History of Philosophy at the Guatemalan National Institute. Sub-

Secretary of the Interior and Justice of the Revolutionary Junta of 1944. President of the Preparatory Session of the National Constituent Assembly of 1945. Secretary General to the President of the Republic. Sub-Secretary of Foreign Relations. President of the National Electoral Commission. Chief of the Department of Publicity and Cultural Extension at the University of San Carlos, and Editor of the University *Bulletin,* 1956-1958. President of the Law School, 1962-1963. Delegate of the Law School to the Superior University Council, 1963-1965. Author of numerous publications dealing with social, political, and legal problems. Member of the Inter-American Bar Association.

Molina Mencos, Carlos.
   Minister of Economy of the Republic of Guatemala, 1970-1974. Born January 2, 1939. Studies at the University of Louisville, and the University of San Carlos. Licenciado in Juridical and Social Sciences from the University of San Carlos, 1964. Chief of the Department of Economics of the Guatemalan Chamber of Industries. Member of the National Commission on Integration. Secretary General of the Federation of Chambers and Associations of Industries in Central America, 1968-1970. Vice Minister of Economy. President of the Mineral Commission of Guatemala. Professor of Industrial Law, Faculty of Engineering, University of San Carlos, 1966-1968. Professor of Law, Rafael Landivar University, Guatemala City.

Ríos Montt, Efraín.
   Presidential candidate of the National Opposition Front and the Christian Democratic Party in the 1974 election. A career military officer, presently holding the rank of Colonel.

Rubio Coronado, Fausto David.
   Minister of Defense of the Republic of Guatemala, 1973-1974. Born September 20, 1928 in Patzún Chimaltenango. A career military officer who graduated from the Guatemalan Polytechnic Institute in 1950. Held various command posts within the Army including Commander of the Presidential Guard, and Chief of the General Staff. Currently holds the rank of General. Became Minister of Defense in 1973 upon the resignation of General Kjell Laugerud García, who resigned to become a candidate for the Presidency.

Sandoval Alarcón, Mario.
   Vice-President of the Republic of Guatemala for the term 1974-1978. Elected in 1974 as the candidate of the National Liberation Party (MLN) and the Institutional Democratic Party (PID), as a running mate of General Kjell Laugerud García. Born May 18, 1923 in Guatemala City. Studied law at the University of San Carlos. Licenciado in Law from the University of Madrid, Spain, 1959. President of the Committee of Anti-

Communist Students, 1954. Founder and Director General of the National Democratic Movement, 1955-1959. Private Secretary to the President of the Junta, Colonel Carlos Castillo Armas, 1954. Director General of the Movement of National Liberation (MLN) 1960 to date. Deputy in the National Constituent Assembly, 1964-1966. Deputy in the National Congress and President of the National Congress, 1970-1974.

Uclés Ramírez, José Trinidad.
Minister of Public Health and Social Assistance of the Republic of Guatemala, 1970-1974. Born May 18, 1924 in Guatemala City. Doctorate in Medicine from the University of San Carlos, 1957. Post-graduate studies in radiology at New York University and Bellevue Medical Center and New York University Hospital. Professor of Physics and Radiology in the Faculty of Medicine at the University of San Carlos. Has held various positions with the General Hospital of Guatemala City heading several of its departments. Also has held office in several Guatemalan Medical Associations, and has represented Guatemala at numerous international medical conferences. Served as President of the Guatemalan Student Association. President of the Political Council of the Institutional Democratic party (PID). Deputy in the National Constituent Assembly of Guatemala, 1965-1966. Deputy in the National Congress of Guatemala, and Chief of the PID Deputies, 1966-1970.

Haiti

Compiled by
Patrick Bellegarde-Smith
Ph.D. Candidate
The American University

Baulieu, Daniel.
Secretary of state for public health since August 1973. Born in Jacmel February 24, 1915. Received his Doctor of Medicine degree in 1938, and further studied radiology in Belgium, 1956-57.

Bayard, Henri.
Under-secretary of state for commerce and industry since August 1973. Received a Law degree from the Faculty of Law, University of Haiti, and studied Business Administration in Canada.

Blanchet, Paul.
Secretary of state for coordination and information since August 1973, and several times previously. Born on June 19, 1915. Until his present assignment, he was Ambassador to Spain.

Bros, Emmanuel.
Secretary of state for finances and economic affairs. Born in Port-au-

Prince, June 7, 1920. Attended the College Saint-Martial, the École Normale d'Instituteurs, and received a Law degree from the Faculty of Law, University of Haiti.

Brutus, Edner.

Secretary of state for national education since October 1970. Born in Jérémie, April 20, 1911. He attended the Faculty of Law, University of Haiti, receiving a Law degree.

Cambronne, Luckner.

Former secretary of state for national defense and interior, until 1972. Former secretary of state for public works, transport and communications, 1960-64, and private secretary to President-for-Life François Duvalier, 1957-60. Currently Ambassador at Large and Inspector of Embassies and Consulates. Born at Arcahaie, October 24, 1930.

Chalmers, René.

Diplomat. Secretary of state for external relations until April 1971. Currently Ambassador to the United States (1971 to present).

de Ronceray, Hubert.

Director, Haitian Center for Research in the Social Sciences and undersecretary of state for national education since January 1972. Born in Petit-Goave, August 20, 1932. Attended the Lycée Petion, Laval University, Canada, Catholic University in Chile. He received a Ph.D. from Laval University (Sociology) in 1971.

Duvalier, Jean-Claude.

President-for-Life, since April 22, 1971, succeeding his father, Dr. François Duvalier, President-for-Life 1957-71. Born July 3, 1951. Attended the College Bird, the Institution Saint-Louis de Gonzague, and the Faculty of Law, University of Haiti.

Duvalier, Simone Ovide.

First Lady of the Republic, from 1957 to the present. Born March 19, 1913, Léogâne. Attended the École Nationale d'Infirmières. Married Dr. François Duvalier on December 23, 1939. Children: Marie-Dénise, Nicole, Simone, Jean-Claude.

Fortune, Fournier.

President, Cour de Cassation (Supreme Court) since October 1973. Attended the Lycée Petion and the Faculty of Law, University of Haiti, receiving a Law degree in 1943.

Fourcand, Serge.

Secretary of state for commerce and industry. Born May 5, 1937. Received doctorates in economics and political science from Geneva, Switzerland.

Francisque, Édouard.
Former secretary of state for finance and economic affairs. Currently Ambassador to France. Born in 1935. Received a doctorate in economics from the Université de Paris.

Germain, Robert.
Under-secretary of state for Public Health and Population since August 1973. Received a Doctor of Medicine degree from the Faculty of Medicine, University of Haiti, and attended the National University of Córdoba, Argentina.

Gousse, Pierre.
Under-secretary of state for external relations. Born in Jacmel, October 21, 1918. Professional educator, pedagogical advisor, College Saint-Martial 1969; formerly Director-General, ministry for external relations, until May 1971.

Hilaire, Baptiste.
Lt. General, Chief of General Staff, Armed Forces of Haiti (Haut Etat-Major), since August 1973. Born in Jacmel March 17, 1928. Attended the College Saint-Martial and the Military Academy, graduating in 1954 as a sous-lieutenant. Former positions include commander, Port-au-Prince penitentiary, assistant Army Chief of Staff.

Jeanty, Aurelien.
Secretary of state for Justice since October 1973. Born in Port-au-Prince, May 8, 1928. Received a Law degree from the Faculty of Law, University of Haiti in 1951.

Leveille, Remiot.
Under-secretary for agriculture, natural resources and rural development since April 1971. Born in Cap Haitien April 8, 1929. Received a degree in agronomy from the University of Haiti in 1951 (Damien) and a Master of Arts degree from Williams College in 1961.

Levèque, Jaures.
Secretary of state for agriculture, natural resources and rural development since April 1971. Attended the Institut Agricole de Damien, 1939-42, receiving degrees in agronomy and veterinary medicine.

Magloire, Paul Eugène.
Former President of the Republic, 1950-56. Born in Cap Haitien, July 19, 1907. Attended the Military Academy, the École de Droit, LL.B. 1939. Former positions include commander of the Palace Guard 1944-48; member, revolutionary junta of 1950.

Nazaire, Breton.
Secretary of state for interior and national defense, since 1973, replacing Roger Lafontant.

Petit, Pierre.
Secretary of state for public works, transports and communications. Received a degree in engineering.

Raymond, Adrien.
Secretary of state for external relations and cults, since April 1971. Born June 30, 1928. Doctor of Medicine, Faculty of Medicine, University of Haiti, 1953. Did further graduate work in public health in Venezuela.

Raymond, Claude.
Lt. General retired. Ambassador to Spain since August 1973. Former Chief of the General Staff (Haut État-Major), Armed Forces of Haiti, until August 1973. Born in Port-au-Prince, April 14, 1930. Attended the Institution Saint-Louis de Gonzague. Graduated from the Mexican Military Academy in 1952.

Salvant, Achille.
Secretary of state for social affairs. Doctor of Medicine.

Honduras

Compiled by
Kenneth J. Grieb, Associate Professor of History and Coordinator of Latin American Studies, Wisconsin State University – Oshkosh

Acosta Bonilla, Manuel.
Minister of the Treasury and Public Finance of the Republic of Honduras, commencing in 1972. Born January 13, 1929 in El Progreso, Yoro. Law Degree from the National Autonomous University of Mexico. Director of the International Office of Civil Aeronautics of Honduras. Director General of Social Assistance in the Ministry of Social Work. Member of the National Electoral Commission. President of the National Elections Council, 1964-1965. Minister of the Treasury and Economy, 1965-1971.

Aguilar Paz, Enrique.
Minister of Public Health and Social Assistance of the Republic of Honduras, commencing in December, 1972. Born February 15, 1931 in Pespire, Choluteca. Doctorate in Medicine from the National Autonomous University of Honduras, 1956. Post-graduate studies in various fields of medicine at the University of Buenos Aires, Argentina, the Faculty of Medicine of Montevideo, Uruguay, the Faculty of Medicine of Córdoba, Argentina, the Institute of Neurosurgery of Santiago, Chile, the Faculty of Medicine of El Salvador, Temple University School of Medicine, Philadelphia, the Faculty of Medicine of the National Univer-

sity of Colombia, the Faculty of Medicine of Costa Rica, the Faculty of Medicine of Panama, and various hospitals in the Federal Republic of Germany. Author of numerous publications regarding medical techniques, which have appeared in various journals and the proceedings of numerous conferences published throughout Latin America. Titular Professor in the Faculty of Medical Sciences, National Autonomous University of Honduras since 1958. Also holds Professorships in Philosophy and Oral Pathology at the same institution. Member of the Directing Council of the Faculty of Medical Sciences at the National Autonomous University of Honduras, 1960-1964. Dean of the Faculty of Medical Sciences of the National Autonomous University of Honduras, 1964-1967. Chief of medical departments at the General Hospital of San Felipe in Tegucigalpa and the Hospital of La Policlínica Comayaguela.

Alcerro Ovila, José Napoleón.
Minister of Public Education of the Republic of Honduras, commencing in December, 1972. Born March 19, 1915 in Marcala. Doctorate in Medicine and Surgery, National Autonomous University of Honduras, 1942. Further studies in Anesthesiology and Ear and Nose diseases at Charity Hospital in New Orleans. Professor of Ear and Nose Diseases and Director of the Department of Anesthesiology, General Hospital of San Felipe, Tegucigalpa, 1949-1955. Has attended numerous medical conferences. Honduran Minister to France, 1955-1956. Honduran Ambassador to France, 1956-1958. President, Honduran Medical Association, 1959. President, Honduran Association of Anesthesiologists, 1960. President of the Central Medical Hospital of Honduras, 1961-1962. A founding member of the National Reformist Movement. Candidate of the National Party for Presidential Designate in the election of 1963, as part of the ticket of Dr. Ramón E. Cruz. Secretary General of the Professional Front of the National Party, 1964. Deputy to the National Constituent Assembly, 1965-1971. Presidential Designate, 1965-1971. Honduran Ambassador to Costa Rica, 1971-1972.

Batres Galeano, César Augusto.
Minister of Foreign Relations of the Republic of Honduras, commencing in 1972. Born October 29, 1934 in Gracias, Lempira. Licenciado in Juridical and Social Sciences, National Autonomous University of Honduras. Professor in Labor Law at the National Autonomous University of Honduras. Previously served as Chief of Protocol of the Ministry of Foreign Relations, and a Justice of the Supreme Court. Secretary General of the First Central American Seminar on Labor Law. President of the Junior Chamber of Commerce Tegucigalpa, 1957. President of the National Association of Industries, 1968. President of the Honduran Institute of Inter-American Culture, 1968. President of the Rotary Club of Tegucigalpa, 1971.

Bennaton Ramos, José Abraham.

Minister of Economy and Commerce of the Republic of Honduras commencing in December, 1972. Born March 15, 1934 in Tegucigalpa. Degree in Economics from the National Autonomous University of Honduras, 1954. M.A. Degree in Economics from the London School of Economics. Economic Advisor to the Minister of Economy. Chief of the Common Market Section, Chief of the Commercial Policy Section, and Deputy Secretary General of the Secretariat of Central American Economic Integration.

Carías Castillo, Tiburcio.

Ambassador to the Organization of American States of the Republic of Honduras commencing in 1972. Previously served as Minister of Foreign Relations during the first administration of President Oswaldo López Arellano, 1963-1972. The son of Tiburcio Carías Andino, President of Honduras, 1932-1948.

Cruz, Ramón Ernesto.

President of the Republic of Honduras, 1971-1972. Born in 1903. Doctorate in Political and Social Sciences, from the National University of Honduras. Served as a Professor at the Law School of the National Autonomous University of Honduras for 30 years, including a term as Dean of the Law School. Member of the Honduran Supreme Court and the International Court of Justice in the Hague. Also served as a Honduran Ambassador to El Salvador. Elected President in 1971 as the candidate of the National Party, heading a National Unity ticket, and served in that position until removed by a coup in 1972.

Escoto Díaz, Raúl Edgardo.

Minister of Natural Resources of the Republic of Honduras, commencing in 1972. Born March 21, 1931. Degrees in Agronomy from the Pan American School of Agriculture and Mississippi State University. Additional studies with the Rockefeller Foundation in Mexico, and Texas A & M University. Eighteen years of service in various positions in the Ministry of Agriculture of the Republic of Honduras, commencing in 1954 and including service as Sub-Director General of Agriculture, Chief of the Division of Agricultural Development, Chief of the Division of Conservation, and Manager of the Department of Development. Also has held numerous positions with the National Development Bank of Honduras, including Director of the Institute of Anthropology and History, and Director of the National Bank of Development. Director of the National Electric Company. Director of the National Agrarian Institute. Director of the Honduran Institute of Coffee. Director of the National Institute for Social Welfare. Has attended numerous conferences on agriculture and developmental matters.

Fonesca Zúñiga, Gautama.
Minister of Labor of the Republic of Honduras, commencing in 1972. Born August 17, 1932 in San Pedro Sula. Law Degree from the National Autonomous University of Honduras, 1957. Governor of the Province of Gracias a Dios. Legal Advisor to the Secretariat for Central American Economic Integration 1964-1970. Legal Advisor to the Central American Bank for Economic Integration, 1970. Minister of Labor of the Republic of Honduras, 1971. Returned to private law practice in 1972 before re-entering the Cabinet later that year.

Hernández Rosa, José de la Cruz.
Chief of the Honduran General Staff, commencing in January, 1971. Born May 3, 1930 in Comayaguela. A career military officer who entered the Army in 1947, and became an officer in 1951. Presently holds the rank of Colonel. Has held numerous command positions within the Army, and served as Honduran representative to the Central American Defense Council from 1966-1967.

López Arellano, Oswaldo.
President of the Republic of Honduras and Commander-in-Chief of the Armed Forces, commencing in December, 1972. Previously served as Chief of State and President 1963-1971. Born June 30, 1921 in Danli El Paraíso. A career military officer who enlisted in the Army in 1939, and was commissioned a Second Lieutenant in 1943. Attended the National Aviation School, and transferred to the Air Force when it became an independent service. Presently holds the rank of General. Minister of Defense, 1956-1963. Commander-in-Chief of the Honduran Armed Forces, 1971 to the present. President of the Republic, 1963-1971, and 1972-1975, when he was overthrown in a scandle involving bribes paid by United Brands for tax concessions.

Melgar Castro, Juan Alberto.
Minister of Government of the Republic of Honduras, commencing in December, 1972. Born June 26, 1930 in Marcala, La Paz. A career military officer presently holding the rank of Colonel. His military career includes service as Assistant to the Chief of Staff of the Honduran Armed Forces, command positions in charge of various military units and military zones within the Republic, and service as Commander of the Special Security Corps during 1972 prior to his appointment as Minister. On April 21, 1974, became president of Honduras after the supreme council of the armed forces ousted Oswaldo López Arellano for his alleged involvement in bribes received from United Brands. He is considered to have close alliances with conservative landowners and the business community. Although conservative politicians supported the overthrow of López Arellano, Melgar and the armed forces have made it clear that they

plan on staying in power "for as long as necessary" in order to bring about agrarian reform and the stimulation of national and foreign investments. The overthrow was supported by young officers sympathetic with the current Peruvian government.

Ramírez, Roberto.

President of the Supreme Court of the Republic of Honduras, commencing in 1972. Born January 15, 1908 in Tegucigalpa. Licenciado in Social and Judicial Sciences from the National Autonomous University of Honduras, 1931. Professor of Mercantile Law at the National Autonomous University of Honduras, 1940 to the present. Additional studies at the National Autonomous University of Mexico, 1943. President of the Central Bank of Honduras, 1950-1961. Member of the Board of Governors of the Central American Bank of Economic Integration from its foundation until 1971, and of the International Monetary Fund, 1971 to the present. Alternate Member of the Board of Governors of the Inter-American Bank of Development, from its foundation until 1971. President of the Honduran Committee for the Alliance for Progress. President of the Central American Institute for Comparative Law, President of the Honduran Society of Attorneys. Member of the Institute of Comparative Law, National Autonomous University of Mexico. Served two terms as President of the Central American Monetary Council. Dean of the Faculty of Law of the National Autonomous University of Honduras. The author of numerous studies on mercantile law.

Ramírez Landa, Pedro Fermín.

Minister of Defense and Public Security of the Republic of Honduras, commencing in 1972. Born May 30, 1923 in Tegucigalpa. A career army officer who entered the Army in 1940, and presently holds the rank of Colonel. Has held various command positions during his military career, and served as Sub-Secretary of Defense and Public Security before becoming Minister. Also served as Honduran Military Attaché in Guatemala and as Honduran delegate to the Permanent Commission of the Central American Council of Defense.

Rivera Bermúdez, Miguel Ángel.

Minister of Communications, Public Works, and Transport of the Republic of Honduras, commencing in 1973. Born May 18, 1916 in San Pedro Sula. Civil Engineering Degree from the National Autonomous University of Mexico. Member of the Tribunal of Honor of the Association of Honduran Civil Engineers, 1967-1968, and 1969-1973, and President of the Association's Board of Directors, 1968-1969. Professor of Algebra, Faculty of Engineering, National Autonomous University of Mexico, 1939-1940. Professor, Faculty of Engineering of National Autonomous University of El Salvador, 1951-1952. Professor of Engineering and Economics, Faculty of Engineering, National

Autonomous University of Honduras, 1964-1972. Service with the Mexican National Office of Roads, 1946-1948, and the National Office of Roads of El Salvador, 1949-1952. Sub-Director of Development of the National Directory of Roads of the Government of Honduras, 1956-1958. Served in various positions with the Honduran Superior Economic Planning Council, 1960-1967, and held several posts in private industry, 1968-1972.

Soto Cano, José Enrique.
Commander of the Honduran Air Force, commencing in May, 1965. Born October 5, 1923 in Olanchito, Yoro. Graduate of the National Autonomous University of Honduras. A career military officer who entered the Army-Air Force in 1941, became an officer in 1945, and transferred to the Air Force when it became an independent branch. Presently holds the rank of Colonel. Has held numerous positions within the Honduran Air Force, including Chief of Training, and Deputy Chief of the Air Force.

Mexico

Compiled by
Marvin Alisky
Professor of Political Science
Arizona State University

Agramont Cota, Félix.
Governor of Territory of Baja California. Born in Baja California in 1917. Degree as agronomist-engineer from National School of Agriculture of Chapingo. During 1958-1961 general administrator for agriculture and livestock-raising for the state of Jalisco. Subdirector for the National Production Agency for Seeds 1961-1970. Appointed as Baja California Territorial Governor by President Echeverría for the term December 1970-December 1976.

Aguirre, Manuel Bernardo.
Governor of state of Chihuahua. Born in Chihuahua. In 1924 a campaigner for Plutarco Calles for president. Mayor of Chihuahua City. Executive officer for the National Federation of Population Organizations of the Institutional Revolutionary Party (CNOP of the PRI). Federal Deputy in Congress. Senator from Chihuahua. Appointed by President Echeverría to cabinet December 1, 1970. Secretary of Agriculture 1970 to January 1974. PRI candidate for Governor of Chihuahua in 1974 for term October 4, 1974 to October 4, 1980.

Alejo, Francisco.
Assistant Minister of Finance and Public Credit, 1970-74. Minister of National Patrimony (Patrimonio Nacional, January 1975-.)

Alemán Valdés, Miguel.

Former President and tourism official. Born in Savula, Veracruz, on September 29, 1900, the son of General Miguel Alemán (1884-1929). Law degree from National Autonomous University of Mexico 1929. State Supreme Court Justice in Veracruz 1935. Senator from Veracruz 1936. Governor of state of Veracruz 1936-1940. Campaign manager for presidential candidate Manuel Ávila Camacho 1939-1940. Secretary of Internal Affairs (Gobernación) 1940-1946. President of Mexico December 1, 1946-December 1, 1952. Investment banker and lawyer. Head of the conservative wing of the PRI. Since 1964 Director of the National Tourism Commission.

Arellano Tapia, Alicia.

Mayor of Magdalena, Sonora. Born in Magdalena in 1932. Degree in dentistry. Federal Deputy in Congress 1963-1964. First woman ever elected to the federal Senate in Mexico; Senator from Sonora 1964-1970. Married to Dr. Miguel Pavlovich. Elected Mayor of Magdalena in July 1973 for the term 1973-1976.

Biebrich Torres, Carlos Armando.

Governor of state of Sonora. Born in Sahuaripa, Sonora, on November 19, 1939. Law degree from the University of Sonora in 1963. Adjunct professor of law, University of Sonora. Secretary of the Municipal Council of Ciudad Obregón, Sonora. Federal Deputy in Congress. Subsecretary of Gobernación, cabinet of President Echeverría. Married to daughter of Raúl Gándara and niece of César Gándara, former Mayor of Hermosillo and former Secretary of State of Sonora. When nominated by PRI in 1973 at age 33, became Sonora's youngest governor.

Becker, Guillermo.

Undersecretary for Industry in the Ministry of Industry and Commerce.

Beteta, Mario Ramón.

Undersecretary for Finance in the Ministry of Finance and Public Credit. Nephew of noted writer, the late Ramón Beteta, executive publisher of *Novedades* daily newspaper.

Bonilla García, Javier.

Director of the government's Tripartite National Minimum Salaries Commission since December 1970.

Bracamontes, Luis Enrique.

Secretary of Public Works. Born in Talpa, Jalisco, in 1923. Engineering degree from National Autonomous University of Mexico (UNAM) 1946. Director of Public Works for UNAM 1950-1952. Subsecretary of Public Works in presidential cabinet 1952-1958. Director of National Commission of Farm-to-Market Roads 1964-1970. Appointed to presidential cabinet December 1, 1970.

Brauer Herrera, Oscar.
Minister of Agriculture and Livestock-raising, appointed to the cabinet by President Echeverría in January 1974, to replace Manuel Aguirre, who had been nominated by the PRI as Governor of Chihuahua.

Bravo Ahuja, Víctor.
Secretary of Public Education. Born in Tuxtepec, Oaxaca, on February 20, 1918. Engineering degree from National Polytechnic Institute (IPN). Graduate study, UNAM. Director Institute of Industrial Research in Monterrey. Academic Dean, Monterrey Institute of Technology. Subsecretary of Public Education in presidential cabinets 1958-1966. Governor of state of Oaxaca December 1968-November 1970. Appointed to presidential cabinet December 1, 1970.

Campillo Sainz, José.
Secretary of Industry and Commerce. Undersecretary of Industry and Commerce from December 1, 1970, until appointed to succeed Carlos Torres Manzo on January 18, 1974.

Canavati, Jorge.
Assistant Director of the Foreign Trade Institute of Mexico (IMCE), a federal government entity created in 1971.

Cano Pereira, Raimundo.
Director of Aeroméxico (formerly Aeronaves de México until 1973), the government-owned national airline. Subdirector of Aeronaves 1964-1970.

Carrillo, Alejandro.
Publisher of the government owned daily newspaper, *El Nacional*. Student, Tulane University. Licentiate from UNAM. Publisher of leftist newspaper *El Popular* 1938-1945. Secretary General of Workers University. National Committee Secretary of Mexican Federation of Labor (CTM). Mexican Ambassador to Egypt. Federal Deputy in Congress 1964-1967. Professor at National Preparatory School and Dean of History Faculty at Superior War College 1968-1969. On January 18, 1968, named publisher of *Nacional*.

Cervantes del Río, Hugo.
Minister of the Presidency. Born in Mexico City on July 4, 1927. Law degree from UNAM 1951. Secretary to General Rodolfo Sánchez Taboada. Director of Internal Administration of Ministry of the Navy. Governor of the Territory of Baja California 1965-1970.

Cuenca Díaz, Hermenegildo.
Secretary of National Defense. Born in Mexico City April 13, 1902.

Military College. Commissioned army lieutenant 1922. Through the ranks to general, last promotion 1958. Commander of the Army. Senator in Congress from state of Baja California 1964-1970. Appointed to the cabinet December 1, 1970.

de la Colina, Rafael.

Ambassador of Mexico to the Organization of American States. Appointed by President Díaz Ordaz and reappointed December 9, 1970, by President Echeverría.

de la Vega Domínguez, Jorge.

Director General of the National Basic Commodities Company (CONASUPO). Born in Comitán, Chiapas, March 11, 1931. Nephew of Senator Belisario Domínguez, hero of the Revolution. Master's degree (Licenciatura) in economics UNAM 1961. Chairman of first Latin American Congress of Economics Students, Mexico City, 1956. President of the Mexican College of Economists 1963. Director of School of Economics of the IPN 1964. Federal Deputy in Congress 1964-1967. Sales Manager of CONASUPO 1968. Director General of Political, Economic, and Social Studies of the PRI 1968-1970.

Díaz Ordaz, Gustavo.

Former President. Born in San Andrés, Puebla, in 1911. Law degree UNAM. Prosecuting Attorney for Municipality of Tehuacán, Puebla. Criminal District Court Judge in Puebla. Justice of state Supreme Court of Puebla. Federal Deputy in Congress. Senator from Puebla 1946-1952. Executive Officer of Ministry of Gobernación 1952-1958. Minister of Gobernación 1958-1964. President of Mexico 1964-1970.

Dovalí Jaime, Antonio.

Director of Petróleos Mexicanos, the governmental petroleum corporation. Born in Zacatecas in 1905. Engineering degree UNAM. Director of School of Engineering UNAM 1959. Director of the National Petroleum Institute. Appointed to the cabinet December 1, 1970.

Ducoing, Luis H.

Governor of state of Guanajuato. Born in San Luis, Guanajuato, in 1937. Law degree University of Guanajuato. Secretary General of Guanajuato state committee of PRI 1962. Federal Deputy and president of Chamber of Deputies 1964-1967. Education Director for National Peasant-Farmers Federation (CNC). Elected governor on July 1, 1973, for the term 1973-1979.

Echeverría, Rodolfo, Jr.

Executive Officer (Oficial Mayor) of the National Executive Committee of the dominant political party, the PRI. Nephew of the President of the Republic. Born in 1940 in Veracruz. Law degree UNAM.

Echeverría Álvarez, Luis.
President of Mexico. Born in Mexico City on January 17, 1922. Law degree from UNAM. Secretary to the president of the National Executive Committee of the PRI 1940-1952. Director of Press and Public Relations for the PRI 1949-1952. Director of Accounts and Internal Administration for the Ministry of the Navy 1950-1954. Administrator of Ministry of Public Education 1954-1957. Undersecretary of Gobernación 1958-1963. Minister of Gobernación 1964-1970. President of the Republic December 1, 1970, to December 1, 1976.

Echeverría Álvarez, Rodolfo.
Director of the government's National Film Bank. Brother of the President of the Republic. Former motion picture actor.

Echeverría Zuno, Álvaro.
Chairman of the Pacific Coast Development Commission. Son of the President of the Republic.

Encinas, Luis.
Director of the government's National Bank of Agricultural Credit. Born in Sonora. Law degree. President of the University of Sonora. Governor of state of Sonora 1961-1967. Bank appointment in January 1971.

Faesler, Julio.
Director of the government's Mexican Institute for Foreign Trade (IMCE). Master's in economics (Licenciado) UNAM. Director of Economic Integration with other Latin American Republics, Ministry of Industry and Commerce 1964-1970. Appointed to IMCE in 1971.

Fernández Hurtado, Ernesto.
President of the Banco de México, the government's federal reserve banking system. Born in Mexico City in 1921. Licenciado in economics UNAM. With the Banco de México since 1945, rising from economic consultant to subdirector to general manager. Appointed bank president December 1, 1970.

Flores, Oscar.
Governor of state of Chihuahua. Elected for the term October 4, 1968 to October 4, 1974. Succeeded by Manuel B. Aguirre.

Flores de la Peña, Horacio.
Minister of National Properties (Patrimonio Nacional). Born in Saltillo, Coahuila, on July 24, 1923. Licenciado in. economics UNAM 1946. Doctoral studies in Washington, D.C., 1947-1949. Mexican delegate to the United Nations. Administrator for Bank of Agricultural Credit, then for Bank for Ejido Credit. Comptroller for Decentralized Govern-

mental Corporations 1959-1970. Consultant for the Economic, Political, and Social Studies Institute of the PRI. Appointed to the cabinet December 1, 1970; resigned January 3, 1975.

Gálvez Betancourt, Carlos.
Director of the Mexican Institute of Social Security (IMSS). Born in Jiquilpan, Michoacán, on February 14, 1921. Law degree. Subdirector for Immigration in Ministry of Gobernación. Director of Juridic Affairs for Gobernación. Undersecretary of Gobernación 1964-1968. Governor of state of Michoacán September 1968 to November 1970. Appointed to cabinet December 1, 1970.

Gómez Villanueva, Augusto.
Director of the Department of Agrarian Affairs and Colonization (DAAC). Born in Aguascalientes on July 23, 1930. Licenciado in social sciences UNAM. Federal Deputy in Congress. Secretary General of the National Peasant-Farmer Federation (CNC) 1967-1968. Senator from Aguascalientes. Appointed to the cabinet December 1, 1970.

Gómez Z., Luis.
Director of the National Railroads of Mexico (Ferrocarriles Nacionales de México), appointed May 7, 1973, upon the resignation of Víctor Villaseñor as FF.CC.NN. Director. Former head of the Railroad Workers Unions Federation.

Guerrero López, Euquerio.
Chief Justice of the federal Supreme Court of Mexico. Law degree from UNAM. Practicing attorney, then judge in the lower courts.

Hank González, Carlos.
Governor of state of México. Education degree. Professor at preparatory schools. Director General of Basic Commodities Company (CONASUPO) 1964-1969. Governor September 1969 to September 1975.

Hirschfeld Almada, Julio.
Director of the federal government's Department of Tourism. Director of Airports December 1, 1970-November 6, 1973. On that date named by President Echeverría to succeed Agustín Olachea as Tourism Director.

Jiménez Cantú, Jorge.
Minister of Public Health and Welfare (SSA). Born in Mexico City on October 7, 1914. Physician with medical degree UNAM. Secretary of Government for state of México 1957-1963. Medical director for Ministry of Communications. Appointed to the cabinet December 1, 1970.

Krieger Vázquez, Emilio.
Director of government-owned heavy-industry complex, Ciudad

Sahagun, site of factories for railroad freight cars, trucks, buses, and diesel engines.

López Portilo, José.
Minister of Finance and Public Credit. Born in Mexico City. Law student University of Chile 1941-1945. Graduate study in law UNAM 1946-1950. Professor of Law UNAM 1948-1958. Director of Federal Material Betterment Boards. Legal Counsel for Ministry of the Presidency 1965-1968. Undersecretary of Ministry of the Presidency 1968-1970. Appointed to the Echeverría cabinet May 30, 1973, to replace Hugo B. Margáin.

Loret de Mola, Carlos.
Governor of state of Yucatán. Born in Yucatán. Senator from Yucatán 1964-1970. Elected Governor for term February 1, 1970 to February 1, 1976.

Madrazo, Carlos.
Federal Deputy in Congress. Law degree. Son of Carlos Madrazo, Sr., the late prominent critic of the government. Madrazo Sr. had been Governor of Tabasco and president of the PRI during 1965, then fired for trying to open party nominations to rank-and-file balloting. Since his father's death in an airplane crash in June 1969, considerable political speculation has focused on Carlos Jr. carrying on his father's career of articulator within the PRI.

Margáin, Hugo B.
Mexican Ambassador to Britain. Born in Mexico City on February 13, 1913. Law degree UNAM, 1937. Director General of Mercantile Taxes of the Ministry of Finance 1951. Director of Income Taxes 1952-1959. Executive Officer of the Ministry of Industry and Commerce 1959-1961. Subsecretary of Industry and Commerce 1961-1964. Mexican Ambassador to the United States 1964-1970. Minister of Finance and Public Credit December 1, 1970, to May 30, 1973. Named an ambassador on June 12, 1973.

Martínez Domínguez, Alfonso.
Former PRI president and former Governor of the Federal District. Born in Monterrey, Nuevo León, in 1922, direct descendant of Revolutionary hero Belisario Domínguez. Bachelor's degree Monterrey Franco-Mexican College. Clerk for Federal District 1935. Editor for Public Relations for Department of Federal District. Federal Deputy in Congress 1943-1946, 1952-1954, 1964-1967. Secretary General of Federation of Unions of Government Employees (FSTSE) 1949-1953. Chairman of U.S.-Mexican Interparliamentary Conference in La Paz, B.C., February 1965. President of the PRI 1966-February 1972. Governor of the Federal District December 1, 1970 to June 14, 1971.

Martínez Domínguez, Guillermo.
Former Director of Nacional Financiera, the government's development bank. Born in Monterrey, Nuevo León, in 1924, brother of Alfonso Martínez Domínguez. Orphaned at 11. Economics degree from UNAM. Professor of Economics UNAM 1948-1964. Columnist for newspaper *Excelsior,* winning 1953 prize for best editorial in a Mexican daily. Director of the Small Business Bank. Executive Officer of Federal Electricity Commission 1955-1959. Director of Federal Electricity Commission 1964-1970. Director of Nacional Financiera December 1, 1970 to January 11, 1973.

Moya Palencia, Mario.
Minister of Gobernación. Born in Mexico City in 1933. Law degree from UNAM. Administrator in public relations, National Railroads 1955-1958. Subdirector of Public Lands in Ministry of National Properties (Patrimonio Nacional) 1959-1964. Director General of Bureau of Cinematography of Ministry of Gobernación December 1964-July 1969. Chairman of Board of Paper Producer and Importer government corporation (PIPSA) 1968-1969. Subsecretary of Gobernación July 1969-November 1969. Acting Minister November 1969. Appointed to cabinet December 1, 1970.

Muñoz Ledo, Porfirio.
Minister of Labor. Replaced Rafael Hernández Ochoa in the Echeverría cabinet. Born in 1933. Undersecretary of Presidency December 1970 to September 1972. Appointed to cabinet September 1972.

Murillo Vidal, Rafael.
Governor of state of Veracruz. Born in Veracruz. Law degree. Senator from Veracruz 1964-1970. Elected Governor for the term December 1968 to December 1974.

Nogueda Otero, Israel.
Governor of state of Guerrero. Born in Guerrero. Law degree. Mayor of Acapulco. Elected to serve the remaining four years of six-year term (1969-1975) of Governor Caritino Maldonado, who was killed in a helicopter crash in April 1971. Governor Nogueda to serve until April 1, 1975.

Olachea Borbón, Agustín.
Mexican Ambassador to Romania. Born in Tijuana, Baja California, on May 2, 1933. Economics degree UNAM. Administrator in Financial Studies Bureau of Ministry of Finance and Public Credit. Coordinator for Economic and Social Programs in PRI presidential campaign of President Adolfo López Mateos in 1957. Consultant for National Border Program. Publisher of *Bureau of Tourism Research* quarterly 1966-1970. Director of

Tourism for federal government December 1, 1970 to November 7, 1973, when appointed Ambassador to Romania.

Orozco Romero, Alberto.
Governor of state of Jalisco. Born in Jalisco. Elected Governor for the term March 1, 1971 to March 1, 1977.

Ovalle Fernández, Ignacio.
Undersecretary of the Presidency Ministry. Born in 1945. Private Secretary to President Echeverría December 1, 1970 to September 16, 1972, when promoted to Undersecretary.

Páez Urquidi, Alejandro.
Governor of state of Durango. Born in Durango. Governor for term September 1968 to September 1974.

Petriccioli, Gustavo.
Undersecretary for Finance in the Ministry of Finance and Public Credit in the Echeverría cabinet.

Portes Gil, Emilio.
Former President of Mexico. Born in Ciudad Victoria, Tamaulipas in 1891. Law degree. Federal Deputy. Governor of Tamaulipas 1925-1928. Minister of Gobernación 1928. President of México 1928-1930. Honorary LL.D. degree from Texas Tech University 1967. Consultant on government-business relations.

Posadas Espinosa, Alejandro.
Executive Director of National Commission for the Corn Production Industry. Born in Mexico City in 1940. Accounting Degree (Contador Público). Administrator of Office of Affiliates of the National Basic Commodities Company (CONASUPO) 1970 to July 1973, when appointed to head the Maíz Commission.

Rabasa, Emilio O.
Minister of Foreign Relations. Born in Mexico City on January 23, 1925, son of Ambassador Oscar Rabasa. Law degree UNAM. Legal counsel for Department of Banking of Ministry of Finance, then for Ministry of Agriculture, then for Ministry of Public Health. Director of government's Bank of Cinematography 1965-1970. Chairman of Board of Churubusco Studios Chain of Motion Picture Theaters. Became Ambassador to the United States September 21, 1970. Appointed to the cabinet December 1, 1970.

Ravize, Manuel A.
Governor of state of Tamaulipas. Born in Tamaulipas. Mayor of Tampico. Elected Governor for term February 1969 to February 1975.

Reyes Heroles, Jesús.
President of the Institutional Revolutionary Party (PRI), Mexico's

dominant party. Law degree. Professor of history UNAM. Director of Petróleos Mexicanos (Pemex) 1964-1970. Chosen head of the PRI in February 1972.

Rodríguez Barrera, Rafael.
Governor of state of Campeche. Born in Campeche February 10, 1937. Law degree University of Campeche 1958. Secretary of Municipal Council of Campeche. Federal Deputy. Elected Governor for the term September 1973 to September 1979.

Rojo Gómez, Javier.
Governor of Territory of Quintana Roo. Born in Huichapan, Hidalgo, in 1897. Law degree. District judge. Director of the National Peasant-Farmer Federation (CNC). Governor of state of Hidalgo. Governor of Quintana Roo 1965-1970. Reappointed by President Echeverría for the term 1970-1976.

Romero Kolbeck, Gustavo.
Director of Nacional Financiera, governmental development bank. Mexican Ambassador to Japan. Director of Financiera Nacional Azucarera until January 11, 1974, when appointed to head NaFin.

Rovirosa Wade, Leandro.
Minister of Hydraulic Resources. Born in Villahermosa, Tabasco, on June 11, 1920. Civil engineering degree UNAM. Chief of planning for the Federal District. Director of Port Construction for the Ministry of the Navy. Directed building of Malpaso Hydroelectric Dam. Appointed to cabinet December 1, 1970.

Sentíes, Octavio.
Governor of Federal District. Law degree UNAM. Appointed Governor on June 14, 1971.

Silva Heroz, Jesús.
Director of the National Workers Housing Fund Institute (INFONAVIT). Economics degrees from UNAM and from Harvard. Professor of Monetary Theory, Colegio de México. Professor of Economics, UNAM. Former economist with research department of Bank of Mexico and with the International Development Bank of Washington.

Torres Manzo, Carlos.
Former Minister of Industry and Commerce. Born in Ticomán, Michoacan, on April 25, 1923. Economics degree UNAM. Doctoral studies in economics, London School of Economics. Diploma at Economic Planner from Economics Institute of Tokyo 1962. Director of Commercial Affairs for Ministry of Industry and Commerce. Director of Internal Administration for National Basic Commodities (CONASUPO).

Appointed to cabinet December 1, 1970, resigning January 18, 1974, and being replaced by Undersecretary José Campillo Sainz.

Zamora Batiz, Julio.
Mexican Ambassador to the Latin American Free Trade Association (LAFTA) in Montevideo, Uruguay.

Zuno Echeverría, María Esther.
President of the National Institute for the Protection of Children. Wife of President Luis Echeverría.

Nicaragua

Compiled by
Kenneth J. Grieb, Associate Professor of History and Coordinator of Latin American Studies, Wisconsin State University – Oshkosh

Buitrago Aja, Mariano.
Minister of the Interior of the Republic of Nicaragua, and President of the Electoral Tribunal of the Department of Managua, 1969-1972. Born August 5, 1912, in Managua. Law degree from the Central Law School of Nicaragua, 1936. Judge of various courts in the city of Managua. Vice Minister of the Interior and of the National District. Minister of Labor and Economics, and Vice-Minister of the Interior, during the administration of President Anastasio Somoza García. Chief of the legal office of the National District during the administration of President Luis Somoza Debayle. Judge of the Supreme Court, 1966-1967. Professor of Criminal and Penal Law at the Central University of Nicaragua. Author of various legal studies.

Guerrero Gutiérrez, Lorenzo.
Minister of Foreign Relations of the Republic of Nicaragua, 1967-1972. Born November 13, 1900 in Granada. Medical degree from the University of the East in Granada. Secretary of the School of Medicine of the East, 1926. Deputy Mayor of Granada, 1930. Mayor of Granada, 1930-1934. Minister of Public Instruction and Physical Education, 1934-1937. Nicaraguan Minister to Mexico, 1937-1942. Private Secretary to the President of the Republic, 1943-1945. Nicaraguan Ambassador to Mexico, 1945-1946. Minister of Public Education, 1946. Member of the Nicaraguan National Constituent Assembly, 1947. Nicaraguan Ambassador to Costa Rica, 1953-1957. Member of the Nicaraguan Senate, 1957-1963. Vice President of the Nicaraguan National Congress, 1960. Vice President of the Republic, 1963-1966, simultaneously serving as Minister of the Interior. Provisional President of the Republic of Nicaragua, 1966-1967. President of the Executive Council of the Organization of Central American States, 1967-1968.

Hueck, Cornelio.

President of the Constituent Assembly of the Republic of Nicaragua, 1972-1974. Born April 18, 1911 in Masaya.

Lovo Cordero, Alfonso.

Liberal Party member of the National Governing Council of the Republic of Nicaragua for the term 1972-1974. Born June 1, 1927, Ocotal. Doctor of Law Degree from the National University of Nicaragua, 1953. Also studied at Cornell University. President of the Board of Directors of the University of León. President of the First University Center of the National University of Nicaragua. President of the First Congress of Student Representatives of the National University of Nicaragua. President of the Central University of Nicaragua delegation to the student conferences at São Paulo and Havana. Founder and President of the Propulsora Agrícola Industrial, S.A., Proprietary Director of the Directive Council of Nicaraguan Development Investments (INDESA), Executive Director of the Nicaraguan Development Foundation (FUNDE). President of the Board of Directors of the National Chamber of Commerce. Vice President of the Board of Directors of the Nicaraguan Agricultural Institute (IAN). President of the National Cotton Commission (CONAL). President of the Nicaraguan delegation to the Inter-American Conference of the International Monetary Fund, Mexico. Has represented the Nicaraguan Government at numerous conferences. Author of various agriculture studies. Minister of Agriculture of Dairying of the Republic of Nicaragua, 1967-1972.

Marín Abaunza, Leandro.

Minister of Government of the Republic of Nicaragua under the National Governing Council, 1972-1974. Born March 7, 1932 in Masaya. Degree in Diplomatic Services from the School of Foreign Service at Georgetown University, Washington. Studied law at the University of the East in Granada, Nicaragua, and political science at St. Joseph's College, Philadelphia, as well as Administrative and International Law at the National University of Panama, and the Ibero-American University in Mexico. Principal Administrative Officer and Secretary General of the Ministry of the National District, 1953. Secretary of the Nicaraguan Embassy in Panama, 1953. Secretary of Legation and Chargé d'Affaires of Nicaragua in Peru, 1954-1956. Counsellor of the Nicaraguan Embassy in Panama, 1956. Counsellor of the Nicaraguan Embassy in Mexico, 1959-1964. Nicaraguan Ambassador to Peru, 1964-1967. Has represented Nicaragua at numerous international and Inter-American Conferences. Vice-Minister of Foreign Relations of the Republic of Nicaragua, 1967-1972.

Martínez Lacayo, Roberto.

Chairman and Liberal Party member of the National Governing Council of the Republic of Nicaragua for the term 1972-1974. Born December

18, 1899 in Granada. A career Military Officer, having served in the National Guard since 1941. Presently holds the rank of Brigadier General. Has held numerous positions in the National Guard, including commander of several Departments of the Republic, and Paymaster General of the National Guard, 1948-1963. Treasurer General of the Republic of Nicaragua, 1963-1968. Director General of the Budget, 1968-1970. Vice Minister of the Treasury and Public Credit, 1970-1972. Minister of Defense, 1972-1974.

Montiel Arguello, Alejandro.
Minister of Foreign Affairs of the Republic of Nicaragua under the National Governing Council, 1972-1974. Born March 13, 1917 in Granada.

Montiel Bermúdez, Gustavo.
Minister of the Economy of the Republic of Nicaragua under the National Governing Council, 1972-1974. Born January 19, 1914 in Juigalpa.

Mora Rostrán, José Antonio.
Alternate member of the National Governing Council of the Republic of Nicaragua and Minister of Public Education, 1972-1974. Born February 25, 1931 in Managua.

Paguaga Irias, Edmundo.
Conservative Party member of the National Governing Council of the Republic of Nicaragua for the term 1972-1974, and Candidate of the Conservative Party for the presidential term 1974-1980. Born June 15, 1923 in Ocotal. Doctor of Law degree from the National University of Nicaragua. Has held numerous positions within the Conservative Party, including Vice President of its National Board of Directors, 1968-1972. A Deputy in the National Congress of Nicaragua, 1967-1972, and in the National Constituent Assembly, 1972-1974.

Somoza Debayle, Anastasio.
Supreme Chief and Commanding General of the Armed Forces of the Republic of Nicaragua, President of the Republic of Nicaragua, 1967-1973, Candidate of the Liberal Party for the presidential term 1974-1980, President of the National Emergency Committee, and Minister of National Reconstruction commencing in 1973, and as such in charge of relief efforts following the December 1972 earthquake and reconstruction of the capital city of Managua. Born December 5, 1925 in León. Son of General Anastasio Somoza García, President of the Republic from 1936-1956, and brother of Luis Somoza Debayle, President of the Republic 1957-1963. Studied at La Salle Military Academy in New York, and graduated from the United States Military Academy at West Point, 1946. Entered the Nicaraguan National Guard as Sub-Lieutenant, on July 1,

1941. Promoted to rank of Captain, 1942; Major, 1946; Colonel, 1948; General of Brigade, 1957; Major General, 1960; and General of Division, 1964. His military career includes service as Inspector General of the Army, 1946-1947; Commander of the First Presidential Battalion, 1947; Commander of the Fifth Battalion in León, 1947; Chief of Operations and Inspector General of the Army, 1947; Director of the Nicaraguan Military Academy, 1948-1950; Chief of the General Staff, 1950-1956; Deputy Director of the Official Journal of the National Guard, 1956-1967. Has headed the Nicaraguan Delegation to numerous international conferences, including Inter-American Conclaves and the United Nations General Assembly.

Sánchez, Heberto.
Minister of Defense of the Republic of Nicaragua under the National Governing Council, 1972-1974. Born December 31, 1922 in Boaco.

Valle Olivares, Luis.
Alternate member to the National Governing Council of the Republic of Nicaragua, Minister of the National District, and Executive Secretary of the National Governing Council, 1972-1974. Born February 7, 1928 in Managua.

Panama

Compiled by
Kenneth J. Grieb, Associate Professor of History and Coordinator of Latin American Studies, Wisconsin State University – Oshkosh

Arias, Ricardo Manuel.
President of the Republic of Panama, 1955-1956, and long time political figure. Born April 4, 1912. Studied at LaSalle College of Panama City, Shenandoah Valley Academy, and Georgetown University. An employee of Inter-American Hotels, 1945. President, Panama Aviation Company, 1946-1955. Minister of Agriculture and Commerce of the Republic of Panama, 1949-1951. Minister of Labor, Public Health and Social Welfare, 1952-1955. Minister of Foreign Relations, 1955. Vice-President of the Republic, 1952-1955.

Barletta, Nicolás Ardito.
Minister of Planning and Economic Development of the Republic of Panama commencing in 1973. Born August 21, 1938 in Aguadulce, Cocle. Studied at LaSalle College of Panama City. Holds bachelor's and master's degrees in Agricultural Engineering from North Carolina State University, and a Ph.D. in Economics from the University of Chicago. Adviser to the Ministry of Economy and Finance and to the Panamanian National Bank during the 1960's. Professor of public finance at the University of

Panama. Director General of Planning and Administration, 1968-1973.

de la Ossa, José Antonio.

Minister of Housing of the Republic of Panama, commencing in 1973. Born August 24, 1931 in Panama City. Studied at LaSalle College of Panama City, the University of Panama and Cornell University. Holds an engineering degree from the University of Panama. An employee of the First National City Bank of New York throughout his early career. Panamanian Ambassador to the United States, 1970-1972.

Fábrega, Edwin Elías.

Minister of Public Works of the Republic of Panama commencing in 1971. Born July 19, 1929. Architecture Degree from the University of Panama, and Master's Degree in City Planning from the University of California. An employee of the Panama Canal Company, 1950-1954. Helped organize and served as an employee of the Ministry of Public Works, 1955-1960. Engaged in private business as head of an architectural firm commencing in 1968.

González, Gerardo.

Minister of Agricultural Development of the Republic of Panama commencing in 1972. Born April 13, 1929, in Santiago, Veraguas. Licenciado in Business Administration from the University of Panama. An employee of the office of Comptroller General of the Republic of Panama for most of his career. Previously served as Vice-Minister of Commerce and Industry.

Jaén, Marcelino.

President of the National Legislative Commission of the Republic of Panama, commencing in 1972. Born April 26, 1919 in Penonome, Cocle. Licenciado in Law from the University of Panama. A secondary school teacher and practicing attorney in Penonome throughout most of his career. Has also served as a correspondent for the Panamanian newspaper *La Hora.*

Lakas, Demetrio Basilio.

President of the Republic of Panama, commencing in January, 1970. Born on August 29, 1925 in Colón. Studied at the Canal Zone Junior College, Texas Wesleyan University, and Texas Technological College. Holds bachelor's degrees in Business Administration and Architectural Engineering. Had a career in private business as an architectural engineer and business executive, prior to his appointment to the Presidency by the Military Junta in January, 1970.

Manfredo, Fernando.

Minister of Commerce and Industries of the Republic of Panama commencing in 1969. Born January 29, 1927 in Panama City. Licenciado in

Economics from the University of Panama. A private businessman for most of his career.

Murgas, Rolando.
Minister of Labor and Social Welfare of the Republic of Panama, commencing in 1972. Born June 12, 1940 in Santiago, Veraguas. Doctorate in Law from the University of Panama, 1969. Law Professor at the University of Panama commencing in 1969.

Royo, Arístides.
Minister of Education of the Republic of Panama, commencing in 1973. Born December 15, 1940 in Oviedo, Spain. Educated in Spain and Italy.

Sánchiz, Miguel A.
Minister of Finance and Treasury of the Republic of Panama commencing in 1972. Born December 25, 1926 in Chitre, Herrera. A graduate of the Pan American Institute of Panama City. Also studies in Accounting at the University of Panama. An officer of the Panamanian Division of the First National City Bank of New York, commencing in the mid-1950s. Served as manager of the bank's branches in David and Colón.

Sucre, Carlos Arturo.
Vice-President of the Republic of Panama, commencing in 1969. Born March 19, 1928 in El Cristo, Cocle. Holds a Law Degree from the University of Panama. His early career was spent in private law practice in the Panamanian capital. An employee of the Financial Affairs Office of the Ministry of Finance and Treasury and Legal Adviser to the City of Panama and to the Institute for Training and Utilization of Human Resources during the 1950s and 1960s. Member of the Directive Council of the University of Panama, commencing in 1969.

Tack, Juan Antonio.
Minister of Foreign Relations of the Republic of Panama commencing in 1970. Born November 16, 1934 in Panama City. Degree in Philosophy and Literature from the University of Panama. A teacher in secondary schools during the 1950s. Professor of History at the University of Panama commencing in 1960. Chief of the America, Africa, Asia and Europe section of the Panamanian Foreign Ministry, 1960-1966. Panamanian Ambassador to France, 1966-1968.

Torrijos Herrera, Omar.
Maximum Leader of the Panamanian Revolution, Chief of State, and Commander in Chief of the Panamanian National Guard. Born February 13, 1929 in Santiago, Veraguas. Graduate of the Military Academy of El Salvador, 1951. Entered service in the Panamanian National Guard in 1952. A career military officer, rising to the rank of Lieutenant Colonel by

1968 when he became Commander in Chief. A member of the junta which took over the government October 11, 1968 in a military coup. Presently holds the rank of Brigadier General. Appointed Maximum Revolutionary Leader and Supreme Chief of the Revolution for a six year term, 1972-1978, by the Assembly of Community Representatives in 1972, which created the position through the new constitution written that year.

Vásquez, Juan Materno.

Minister of Government and Justice of the Republic of Panama. Born September 14, 1927 in Nombre de Dios, Colón. Licenciado in Law from the University of Panama, 1954. Engaged in private law practice throughout most of his career.

Paraguay

Compiled by
Rand Dee Bowerman
Graduate Research Associate
Center for Latin
American Studies
Arizona State University

Nogués, Alberto.

Foreign Minister of Paraguay 1974.

Sapena Pastor, Raúl.

Chief, National Administration of Electricity of Paraguay. Chairman of the negotiating team for the Itaipu hydroelectric project.

Stroessner, Alfredo.

President of Paraguay. Born in 1913 in Asunción. Chief of Staff of the Army 1950-54. Led coup that seized power in May 1954, and officially became President August 15, 1954. Promulgated new constitution in 1967 and was elected for his fifth term in August of 1974. Stimulated contacts with Brazil that have led to the present construction of the giant Itaipu hydroelectric plant on the upper Paraná.

Peru

Compiled by
Philip D.S. Gillette, Department
of Sociology and Coordinator,
Academic Programs, Latin
American Center, University
of California, Los Angeles

Alva Orlandini, Javier.

The new secretary general of Acción Popular (1974), he was ordered deported and the party banned on May 31, 1974.

Arce Larco, José.

Born in Salaverry, Peru, on October 28, 1917. Married to Victoria

Cánepa, five children. Graduated Escuela Naval, December 31, 1939, and commissioned ensign, January 1, 1940. He was promoted to rear admiral on January 1, 1968, and to vice admiral on January 1, 1974. He has attended the Centro de Altos Estudios Militares (CAEM). Admiral Arce has served as commander of the Fluvial Force of the Amazon and chief of the 5th Naval Zone (1968), chief of the Naval General Staff, Inspector General of the Navy (1970-71), commander of the Auxiliary Fleet, commanding officer of the cruiser *BAP Almirante Grau*, sub-director and chief of studies of the Escuela Superior de Guerra Naval, Naval Attaché to the U.S. and OAS, Peruvian Naval Delegate to the Inter-American Defense Board (April 1, 1971) and, on May 30, 1974, as commander of the Navy and Minister of the Navy in the Revolutionary Government.

Arróspide Mejía, Ramón.
   Born in Ascope, La Libertad, Peru on November 3, 1921. Married to Rosario Jiménez, four children. Graduated from the Escuela Naval in December, 1941 and commissioned ensign on January 1, 1942. He was promoted to rear admiral on January 1, 1972. Admiral Arróspide has served as the Naval representative on the consultative committee on the law of the sea in the Ministry of Foreign Relations, commander of the submarine flotilla, Naval Attaché in England, secretary general to the commander of the Navy, commander of the Fluvial Force of the Amazon, and director of the Escuela Superior de Guerra Naval. On January 1, 1972 he was appointed Minister of Housing. He resigned in May 1974 in protest to the forced resignation of Vice Admiral Luis E. Vargas Caballero, the Minister of the Navy, in a dispute over freedom of the press.

Arias Stella, Javier.
   Born in Lima in 1925. Married to Nancy Castillo. Graduated from the National University of San Marcos in Medicine. Served as Minister of Public Health from July 28, 1963 to September 13, 1965 and again from September 7, 1967 to May 29, 1968, when he was appointed Minister of Government, serving until October 2, 1968, when the entire cabinet resigned. As an early member of the Acción Popular party of former President Belaúnde, Arias rose to the position of secretary-general of the party in the early 1970s. Since the Revolutionary Military Government took power, Arias has served as one of the spokesmen of Acción Popular, and has been deported several times as a result of his criticisms of the military government, the last time being on May 25, 1974.

Bernos Díaz, Miguel.
   Married to María Accinelli García Rada, eight children. Graduated from the Escuela Naval on December 29, 1945, and commissioned ensign on January 1, 1946. He was promoted to rear admiral on January 1, 1974. Admiral Bernos has been commanding officer of four Peruvian naval

vessels including the cruiser *BAP Coronel Bolognesi,* commanded the Naval Training Center and the Naval Arsenal, and was appointed Director of Naval Intelligence in January 1974. He is a graduate of the CAEM.

Bedoya Reyes, Luis.

Born in Callao in 1919. Married to Laura Vivanco. Graduated from the National University of San Marcos in law. Director General of Information in the government of José Luis Bustamante y Rivero in 1948. A founding member of the Partido Demócrata Cristiano, he has served as secretary-general of the party. Minister of Justice and Religion from July 28, 1963 to October 25, 1963, when he resigned to head the AP-DC ticket as candidate for mayor of Lima in the 1963 municipal elections. He was elected and served from December 1963 until the end of a second term in December 1969. Since the ouster of President Belaúnde, Bedoya has defended the record of Belaúnde.

Belaúnde Terry, Fernando.

Born in Lima on October 7, 1912. Married to Carola Aubry (divorced), and in April 1970 to Violeta Correa Miller. Two children. Graduated from the University of Texas in architecture in 1935. Joined the Club Nacional in 1938. Served as a member of congress, 1945-48. Dean of the Faculty of Architecture, National Engineering University, 1955-60. Candidate for the Presidency of Peru, 1956, 1962. Founded the Acción Popular party in 1957. Elected President of Peru in 1963, and assumed office on July 28, 1963. A visionary who planned to modernize Peru through grand public works and moderate reforms, Belaúnde's goals were thwarted by an opposition Congress and ultra-conservative sectors of the economy. He was overthrown by the military high command on October 3, 1968. At present he is living in the United States. He has been a visiting professor of urban planning at George Washington University, Georgetown University, Harvard and Columbia.

Benavides Benavides, José.

Born on May 21, 1920 in Lima. Son of former President Marshal Oscar R. Benavides. Married to Rosa Gubbins Hercelles. Graduated at the head of his class from the Escuela Militar de Chorrillos in 1940, and was commissioned a sub-lieutenant in infantry. He was promoted to brigadier general on January 1, 1966. He has had further military school at the French Military Academy at St. Cyr and the U.S. Infantry Course at Fort Benning, Georgia and the U.S. Armored Course at Ft. Knox, Kentucky. He joined the Club Nacional in 1944. In 1966, he became chief of the Army Intelligence Service, and served as commanding general of the 5th Military Region and as Prefect of the Department of Iquitos from 1967 to 1968. On October 3, 1968 he was appointed Minister of Agriculture in the Revolutionary Military Government, a post in which he served until June 12, 1969, when he resigned in opposition to the agrarian reform policies of the government. He then became Director of Logistics for the Army. During this time, he was a member of a Peruvian agricultural mission to the United Arab Republic and to Israel.

Barandiaran Pagador, Luis M.

An Air Force officer, promoted to major general on January 1, 1968 and to lieutenant general on January 1, 1974. He was director of the Oficina Nacional de Integración in charge of the Andean Common Market affairs. On January 8, 1974 he became Minister of Commerce.

Briceño Zevallos, Gonzalo.

Born in Mollendo, Peru, on March 16, 1923. Married to Gloria Galdós, four children. After six months of study at the National University of San Marcos, he entered the Escuela Militar de Chorrillos, graduating in 1943, second in his class. He was commissioned a sub-lieutenant in infantry on February 1, 1943. He received further military training at the Artillery Course, Ft. Gulick, Canal Zone, the Escuela Superior de Guerra, the Ranger Course, Ft. Benning, Ga., and the CAEM. A specialist in ranger tactics, he commanded the Peruvian Ranger School (Escuela de Comandos) from 1962 to 1964 and commanded the ranger unit that occupied the Presidential palace during the military coup that overthrew President Manuel Prado y Ugarteche on July 18, 1962. He has served as Military Attaché to France, commander of the Republican Guard from 1970 to 1972, commander of the 1st Motorized Infantry Division in Tumbes during 1972, and the 1st Armored Division, in Lima, from April 1973. He was promoted to brigadier general on January 1, 1970.

Carpio Becerra, Alfredo.

Graduated from the Escuela Militar de Chorrillos and commissioned subteniente in the infantry in January 1940. Promoted to division general on January 1, 1971. He graduated from the Escuela Superior de Guerra in 1951. From January 1969 to 1970 he was commander of the 2nd Military Region. In 1970 he was appointed director general of the Oficina Nacional de los Pueblos Jóvenes (ONDEPJOV), in charge of the control and development of the "pueblos jóvenes" or shanty-towns which surround most of the major cities. On April 28, 1971 he was appointed Minister of Public Education.

Cavero Calixto, Arturo.

Born May 27, 1917 in Iquitos. Married to Juana Zavala Pérez, three children. Graduated from the Liceo La Inmaculada in Lima in 1936, and from the Escuela Militar de Chorrillos in 1940. He was commissioned a sub-lieutenant in the cavalry on February 1, 1940. He attended the French Military Academy at St. Cyr from July 1938 to November 1939, as well as the French Command and Staff College in Paris and the U.S. Industrial College of the Armed Forces course in the economics of national security in 1961. He graduated from the CAEM in 1965. A member of the "earthquake" generation, Cavero has been very influential in the circle of officers advising President Velasco. He was promoted to brigadier general on January 1, 1966 and division general on January 1, 1972. He has served as commander of the 7th Infantry Division from Jan. 1966 to Dec. 1967 and then as director of Army Intelligence until Jan. 1970, during which time he headed the COAP — Comité de Asesoramiento de la Presidencia de la República. In 1970 he became Deputy Commandant and Director of Academic Studies of the CAEM, and in January 1971, became Director of the CAEM. In January 1972, General Cavero assumed command of the 3rd Military Region in Arequipa and a year later, was appointed President of the Joint Command of the Armed Forces.

Cornejo Chávez, Héctor.

Born in Arequipa, and a graduate in law from the Universidad de San Agustín in Arequipa, Cornejo Chávez has long been involved in the political arena in Peru as a leader of the Partido Democrático Cristiano (PDC). From 1945 to 1948 he was the personal secretary to President José Luis Bustamante y Rivero and later represented Arequipa in the Chamber of Deputies (1956-62), during which time he was secretary-general and later president of the PDC. In both 1962 and 1963 he was a candidate for the Presidency. Although unsuccessful in both races, he was elected Senator from Lima in 1963, serving until 1968. During this time, he has served as a professor of law at the Universidad Católica in Lima.

Cruzado Zavala, Julio.

Secretary General, Confederación de Trabajadores del Perú (CTP).

de la Flor Valle, Miguel Ángel.

Born on March 11, 1924 in Ferreñafe, and married to María Luisa Illich Remotti, he has four children. Following secondary education at the Colegio Nacional San José in Chiclayo, he entered the Escuela Militar de Chorrillos, graduating in 1945. He was commissioned a subteniente in the infantry on January 1, 1946. On January 1, 1972 he was promoted to brigadier general. In addition to studying at the Escuela Superior de Guerra in 1957-58, he studied for a year at the Superior War College in Paris, France (1959-60). From October 1968, he has been one of President Velasco's key advisors, serving on the COAP from 1968 to 1969. In July 1969 he was elected president of the Peruvian Telephone Company. During 1971 he was commandant of the Centro de Instrucción Militar del Perú (CIMP). On January 1, 1972 he was appointed Minister of Foreign Relations.

de la Jara Ureta, José.

A chief advisor to ex-President Belaúnde, he was secretary-general of Acción Popular when the coup occurred. Deported February 13, 1969.

Duharte, Raymundo.

The President of the Sociedad Nacional de Industrias (SNI) in 1973. His opposition to the economic policies of the military government brought about an order preventing his return to Peru from a business trip in November 1973. On January 8, 1974, a Peruvian lower court denied a writ of habeas corpus and he remains outside the country.

Durán Rey, Rafael.

Born on October 24, 1922, in Lima. Married to Consuelo Padros Puente, four children. Graduated from the Escuela Naval and commissioned ensign in December 1942. Promoted to rear admiral on January 1, 1971. Completed two specialized courses in the U.S. as well as the CAEM in 1967. During 1970 he was commander of the Antisubmarine Flotilla. Subsequently he served as chief of plans, policies and strategy on the Navy General Staff (from January 1971) and later as commander of the cruiser division (1972). He was appointed naval attaché to the U.S. on July 1, 1974.

Fernández Maldonado Solari, Jorge.

Born in Ilo on May 29, 1922. Married to Estela Castro Fauchaux. After attending the Colegio Nacional de Guadalupe, he entered the Escuela Militar de Chorrillos, graduating 8th in his class and commissioned a subteniente in January 1943. His career has been mainly in infantry and intelligence assignments. From 1959 to 1961 he was military attaché in Buenos Aires. Following the 1968 military coup, he was appointed chief of Army intelligence, serving until his appointment as Minister of Energy and Mines, effective March 3, 1969, having been promoted to brigadier general on January 1, 1969, and division general on January 1, 1973. General Fernández Maldonado read the first proclamation of the military government on October 3, 1968 and on October 9, the decree expropriating the International Petroleum Company oil holdings. General Fernández Maldonado is one of the "inner circle" of close advisors to President Velasco, being a member of the "earthquake" generation of colonels who serve as key advisors to the president.

Gallegos Venero, Enrique.

Born on August 4, 1924, in Cuzco. Married Dora Rodríguez Carpi; three children. After attending the Colegio Guadalupe he entered the Escuela Militar de Chorrillos, graduating first in his class (infantry section), in 1945, and commissioned subteniente on December 31, 1945. He was promoted to brigadier general on January 1, 1971. He attended the General Staff Course of the General Staff School in Paris, France in 1957 and the Superior War School, in Paris, from September 1958 to June 1960. General Gallegos served as the coordinator of agrarian reform programs for the military junta that ruled Peru in 1962-63. From 1967 to

1971, he was Chief, Army Intelligence Service. In 1971 he was assigned as commander, 6th light infantry division after having served as assistant minister of the interior from 1969. In January 1972 he was appointed Director, National Intelligence Service. As a colonel, he was the officer who personally arrested then President Belaúnde on October 3, 1968, escorting him from the Presidential Palace. He has been described as a "most revolutionary" officer, one of the "inner circle" of advisers to President Velasco.

Gálvez Velarde, Augusto.

A vice admiral in the Peruvian Navy, he was appointed Minister of Housing on June 5, 1974, replacing Admiral Arróspide Mejía, who resigned as a result of a split with the military government over policies on freedom of the press.

Gilardi Rodríguez, Rolando.

Born on August 31, 1921, in Arequipa. Married first to Ernestina Salavérry Ramos, from whom he was divorced in July 1970. In 1972 he married María García Charme. He has five children. Graduated from the Colegio Nacional in Arequipa, he attended the Escuela Militar de Chorrillos, graduating in 1942 and commissioned a subteniente on August 15, 1942. He was promoted to major general in the Air Force on January 1, 1965 and to lieutenant general on January 1, 1969. He had flight training at the U.S. Naval Air Station, Corpus Christi, Texas in 1942-43. Following assignment as Air Force attache in Washington in 1962-63, he served as acting Inspector General of the Air Force during 1963, and became Secretary-General of the Air Ministry in 1964. He successively served as Director, Air Officers Academy (1966), Deputy Chief of Staff for Training (1967) and was Director of Administration for the Air Force when the military government assumed power in October 1968. On October 3, 1968 he was appointed Minister of Labor and Community Affairs, serving only until November 4, when he was appointed Minister of the Air Force and Commanding General of the Air Force.

Graham Hurtado, José.

Born in Arequipa in 1918, he is married to Carmen Rosa Ayllón. He graduated from the Escuela Militar de Chorrillos in 1941, seventh in his class in the infantry section. He graduated from the CAEM in 1967. He was promoted to brigadier general on January 1, 1969. Shortly after the military coup in 1968, he was appointed Prefect of Lima, serving until March 1969 when he was chosen to head the COAP, which he still heads. He is considered to be one of the "inner circle" of officers who serve in key advisory positions.

Guabloche Rodríguez, José.

Born in San Martín, in 1922. He graduated from the Escuela Militar de

Chorrillos in 1944, and was commissioned a subteniente in artillery in 1944. He has served primarily in intelligence and artillery posts, and was appointed as commandant of the Army Intelligence School in 1967. Since the 1968 coup, he has served as Director General of the Ministry of Education. He was promoted to brigadier general on January 1, 1973.

Gagliardi Schiaffino, José.
Born in Cañete on February 2, 1916. Married to Minnie Wakeham Dasso. Educated at the Royal Air Force Academy, Caserta, Italy, where he received flight training and his "wings" in 1940. A member of the "Italian Club," the group of Air Force officers who received their early training in Italy. During the military government of 1962-63, he served as Minister of Labor and Indian Affairs. In 1965 he was the subchief of the Air Force General Staff, and was promoted to chief of the Air Force General Staff in January 1966. In January 1967 he was appointed Commanding General of the Peruvian Air Force, a post he held until September 7, 1967, when he was appointed Minister of Aviation. His objection to the overthrow of President Belaúnde brought about his resignation on October 3, 1968. One of the more controversial generals in recent Peruvian history, Gagliardi's nomination for promotion to lieutenant general was opposed by the Peruvian Senate in late 1964. He was eventually promoted to that rank on January 1, 1966.

Haya de la Torre, Víctor Raúl.
Born in Trujillo on February 22, 1895. Unmarried. Attended both the Universidad Nacional de Trujillo (1915) and San Marcos (1917), but graduated from neither. While at San Marcos, he was president of the Federación de Estudiantes and was one of the leaders of the 1919 student-workers strike. During a government imposed and subsidized exile from 1923, he founded the first truly disciplined and well-organized political party in Peru, the APRA, which was founded in 1924 in Mexico City as a continental anti-imperialistic, socialist party. He has been the leader of APRA since then and served as its presidential candidate in those elections when APRA was legal — 1931, 1962, and 1963. As leader of the largest party in Peru, he has had a profound influence on Peruvian political life. In recent years, APRA has changed its ideological position markedly to the right. Although remaining the titular and spiritual leader of APRA, Haya spends most of his time in Paris, leaving party affairs to the elected party leadership.

Jiménez del Lucio, Alberto.
A graduate of the U.S. Naval Academy in 1945, Jiménez de Lucio was promoted to rear admiral on January 1, 1971. He has had graduate training at MIT in 1953-56 and again in 1967. His career has been in the engineering and research field, and he served as chief of the office of

research and development of the Peruvian Navy in 1967. From January 1969 to April 1971 he was chief of the Servicio Industrial Marítima (SIMA), the Peruvian Navy shipbuilding agency. On April 27, 1971 he was appointed Minister of Industry and Tourism.

Landázuri Ricketts, Juan.

Born in Arequipa in 1913 and educated at the Universidad de San Agustín in Arequipa, subsequently entering the priesthood. He became Archbishop of Lima in 1955, and was made a cardinal in 1962. His sister is married to the former premier and minister of war, General Ernesto Montagne.

León Velarde, Enrique.

One of the leading civilian supporters of President Velasco. At one time, mayor of San Martín de Porras, a "pueblo joven" suburb of Lima (where his family is a major landowner), León Velarde served for several years as president of Mutual Metropolitana, a large savings and loan association, having resigned his post at Director General of Gobierno Interior to assume that post. The alleged use of Mutual funds for the development of several large housing developments in San Martín de Porras, on family land, caused an investigation and the eventual removal of León Velarde on technical grounds. In July 1974, following an intensive government investigation, President Velasco strongly defended his friend and he was later reinstated.

Marco del Pont Santisteban, Guillermo.

A graduate of the Escuela Militar de Chorrillos in 1944 and a student at the Escuela Superior de Guerra in 1952-53, he was promoted to brigadier general in January 1970 and to division general in January 1974. He served for several years as director of the National Planning Institute, and became Minister of Economy and Finance on January 8, 1974. In July 1974, he resigned his post, citing reasons of health for his action.

Meneses Arata, Raúl.

Born on June 19, 1926 in Arequipa. Married to María Caridad Nugent, he has two children. He graduated from the Escuela Militar de Chorrillos and was commissioned subteniente in engineering in 1948. He was promoted to brigadier general on January 1, 1973. He has attended the Escuela Superior de Guerra (1958-59), and the U.S. Command and General Staff School, Ft. Leavenworth, Kansas. He has served as military attaché to Brazil, chief of the coordinating group for national development of the Army General Staff, and was a member of the COAP for four years prior to his appointment as Minister of Transport and Communications on January 1, 1973.

Mercado Jarrín, Edgardo.

Born in Barranco on September 19, 1919. Married to Gladis Neumann

Terán, they have five children. General Mercado has had extensive training prior to assuming his post as Prime Minister and Minister of War on February 1, 1973. He graduated from the Escuela Militar de Chorrillos in 1940. He attended the Escuela Superior de Guerra (1952-53), the U.S. Command and General Staff School, Fort Leavenworth, Kansas (1956-57), and the Inter-American Defense College, Washington, D.C. in 1964. He was promoted to division general on January 1, 1970. He was director of Army Intelligence from January 1966 until January 1968 when he became the commandant of the Centro de Instrucción Militar del Perú, a post in which he served until the military coup in October. On October 3, 1968 he was appointed Minister of Foreign Relations, a post in which he remained until he became chief of the Army General Staff on January 3, 1972. On February 1, 1973, he became Prime Minister, Minister of War and Commanding General of the Army. General Mercado is considered by many to be the heir apparent to President Velasco, if and when he steps down.

Meza Cuadra Cárdenas, Aníbal.

Born in Bolívar, La Libertad, on August 12, 1920. Married to María Luisa Araoz, with two children. He graduated from the Escuela Militar de Chorrillos in 1941 and was commissioned a subteniente in artillery on January 9, 1941. He was promoted to brigadier general on January 1, 1969. In addition to attending the Escuela Superior de Guerra (1952-53), he has been a student at the U.S. Army Ordnance School (1957-58), and the Centro de Altos Estudios Militares (CAEM) in 1967. He served as military attaché to Ecuador from 1962 to 1964. At the time of the military coup in 1968 he was subdirector of training on the Army General Staff. In October 1968 he became a member of the COAP, serving until April 1, 1969, when he was appointed Minister of Transport and Communications, a post in which he served until January 1, 1973. General Meza Cuadra has been one of the most influential of President Velasco's advisors, one of the "inner circle" surrounding the President.

Miró Quesada de la Guerra, Luis.

Born on December 5, 1880 in Lima. Son of the founder of *El Comercio*, Peru's leading newspaper. Married to Elvira Garland. A graduate in law from the Universidad de San Marcos in 1905. He served as a Diputado representing Tumbes in the period 1906-12, and as mayor of Lima from 1916 to 1918. He served as Dean of the Faculty of Letters of San Marcos in 1925-26 and served as minister of foreign relations in 1931-32. As director of *El Comercio* since the 1935 assassination of his father, he has led the newspaper in vigorous opposition to Haya de la Torre and APRA (his father having been assassinated by an Aprista), and in favor of the nationalization of the International Petroleum Company's (IPC) oil fields at La Brea y Pariñas. Since the military coup in 1968, *El Comercio* has become increasingly opposed to the direction and policies of the Velasco regime. On July 26, 1974, *El Comercio,* along with the other major Peruvian daily newspapers, was taken over by the government and new editors appointed. *El Comercio* is now the property of the National Campesino Federation and is edited by Héctor Cornejo Chávez, a leading Christian Democrat and former candidate for the Presidency. Miró Quesada was placed under house arrest, where he remains at this writing.

Montagne Sánchez, Ernesto.

Born on August 18, 1916 in Lima, the son of General Ernesto Montagne Markholz, a former prime minister (1937-39). Married to Isabel Landázuri Ricketts, sister of the Archbishop of Lima; two children. He graduated from the Escuela Militar de Chorrillos and was commissioned a subteniente in the infantry on February 1, 1938. He was promoted to brigadier general on January 1, 1963 and division general on January 1, 1968. He retired in January 1973. General Montagne's military training includes the Escuela Superior de Guerra (1948-49), the U.S. Command and General Staff School, Ft. Leavenworth, Kansas (1950-51), and the CAEM (1960). He was military attaché to Chile from 1955 to 1957. During the military junta that ruled Peru in 1962-63, he was Prefect of Lima. During 1963 he was commander of the 3rd Military Region and the 3rd Light Infantry Division in Arequipa. From October 3, 1964 to July 31, 1965 he was Minister of Public Education. Upon returning to military duties, he became commandant of the Escuela Superior de Guerra, until January 1, 1967. After a year as Deputy Chief of the Army General Staff, he was appointed commander of the 1st Military Region in Piura, from January 1 to June 5, 1968, when he became Inspector General of the Army, serving until the military coup. On October 3, 1968 he was appointed Prime Minister, Minister of War, and Commanding General of the Army, as well as serving as President of the Armed Forces Joint Command from October to December 1968.

Montero Rojas, Eduardo.

Born on November 2, 1918, at Yurimaguas. Married to María Montalván; four children. After two years of military training at the Royal Military Academy, Caserta, Italy (1937-39), he was commissioned a subteniente in the Air Force on February 1, 1942. He was promoted to major general on January 1, 1963 and lieutenant general on January 1, 1970. His advanced training has included flight training at the U.S. Naval Air Station, Corpus Christi, Texas (1942), the Latin American School, Albrook Air Force Base, Canal Zone (1950), and the Squadron Officers School and Field Officers School, Maxwell Air Force Base, Alabama (1951-52). He was superintendent of the Peruvian Air Force Academy and commander of the Las Palmas Air Base in 1963-65. He was appointed air attaché in Washington, D.C. on January 7, 1965, serving until December

1966, when he served a year as Director General of Meteorology. From October 3, 1968, he was Minister of Public Health and Social Welfare, serving until January 1, 1970, when he became President of the Joint Command of the Armed Forces.

Morales Bermúdez Cerruti, Francisco.

Born in Lima in 1921. Married to Rosa Pedraglio. Graduated from the Escuela Militar de Chorrillos and commissioned subteniente in engineering in January 1943. A graduate of the Escuela Superior de Guerra and CAEM (1967). He was promoted to brigadier general on January 1, 1968 and to division general on January 1, 1972. He served as President Belaúnde's Minister of Finance and Economy from March 19 to May 31, 1968, when he returned to Army duty as Director of Logistics on the Army General Staff. In February 1969 he was again appointed Minister of Finance and Commerce, serving until January 1, 1974, when he was appointed commanding general of the Army. He is next in line to become Prime Minister, Minister of War and commander-in-chief of the Army on January 1, 1975. A member of the "earthquake" generation of officers, Morales Bermúdez is widely respected for his economic expertise, although his orthodox economic views have kept him from being one of the "inner circle" of advisers to President Velasco. He is credited with designing the agrarian reform program.

Richter Prada, Pedro.

Born on January 4, 1920 in Ayacucho. Married to Laura Valdivia. Graduated from the Escuela Militar de Chorrillos and commissioned subteniente in January 1946. He was promoted to brigadier general on January 1, 1971. General Richter Prada was a student at the Armored Officer Advanced Course, U.S. Army Armor School, Fort Knox, Kentucky in 1955-56, and was a student at the Escuela Superior de Guerra in 1952-53 and the CAEM in 1965. He was military attaché in La Paz, Bolivia in 1961-62. In 1966, he served as director of public relations for the Peruvian Army, and became a member of the COAP in 1970. In January 1971 he was appointed Director, National Intelligence Service, serving until his appointment on May 18, 1971 as Minister of the Interior.

Rodríguez Figueroa, Leónidas.

Born in Cuzco. Graduated from the Escuela Militar de Chorrillos and commissioned subteniente in the infantry in January 1944. Promoted to brigadier general on January 1, 1970. He is a member of the "inner circle" of key advisors to President Velasco, having been an original member of the COAP, and perhaps the most influential member of that group. From January 1970 to 1972 he was commanding general of the 1st Armored Division in Lima. He then became Chief of SINAMOS, the Sistema Nacional de Apoyo de Movilización Social. SINAMOS is the Peruvian military government's agency for social mobilization. Following considerable rural unrest and criticism of SINAMOS, Rodríguez was reassigned in January 1974 as commanding general of the 1st Military Region in Lima.

Ruiz Eldredge Rivera, Alberto.

A leading lawyer and politician, Ruiz Eldredge was one of the founders of the Movimiento Social Progresista (MSP) and was its Presidential candidate in the 1962 elections. In 1969-70 he served a term as Decano of the Colegio de Abogados. In March 1970 he was appointed Ambassador to Brazil, a post he held until July 1974 when he was appointed director of *Expreso,* one of the Lima daily newspapers reorganized then. Ruiz Eldredge has been an influential civilian advisor to President Velasco Alvarado.

Sala Orosco, Pedro.

An Air Force officer, promoted to major general on January 1, 1965 and lieutenant general on January 1, 1971. From 1965 to January 1968 he was director of operations for the Peruvian Air Force. He served as director of civil aviation from January 1968 until his appointment as Minister of Labor on September 30, 1970. He was elected President of the International Labor Organization for the 1974-75 term.

Segura Gutiérrez, Eduardo.

Born in Lima on December 16, 1921. Married to Antonieta Jiménez; three children. He graduated from the Escuela Militar de Chorrillos and was commissioned a subteniente in the infantry January 1, 1946. He was promoted to brigadier general on January 1, 1972. He attended the Escuela Superior de Guerra in 1954-55. General Segura was director of the National Intelligence Service from 1969 to 1971. During 1971 he served as a member of the COAP, and was responsible for several Velasco government programs, including the investigation of corruption in the Belaúnde government, the planning of municipal government, and the program to enhance the public image of the Velasco government. In January 1972 he was appointed commanding general of the Centro de Instrucción Militar del Perú and in April 1972, was elected president of the Peruvian Telephone Company. In April 1974 he was appointed as the director of the newly established National Information Service. General Segura was one of the "earthquake" generation of colonels who supports Velasco, and he has become one of the "inner circle" of key advisors.

Seoane Corrales, Edgardo.

Born in Chorrillos on May 15, 1903. A graduate of the National Agrarian University. Married to Rosa Weiss. In 1963 he was executive director of the National Office for the Promotion of Agrarian Reform. He was elected First Vice President of the Republic on the Acción Popular ticket with Fernando Belaúnde Terry in 1963, taking office on July 28.

From June 1967 to 1969 he was secretary-general of Acción Popular, and was chosen as the party's 1969 presidential candidate following a split with Belaúnde over policy. From September 7, 1967 to November 16, 1967 he was Prime Minister and Minister of Foreign Relations in the Belaúnde government, as well as Ambassador to Mexico. A supporter of the Velasco regime, he has served in an advisory capacity to President Velasco and as President of the Banco de Fomento Agroprecuario since August 1973. His brother, Manuel, was a leading member of the Aprista party until his death.

Tantaleán Vanini, Javier.

Born in Chiclayo in 1920. Graduated from the Escuela Militar de Chorrillos and commissioned subteniente in January 1941. He studied at the Escuela Superior de Guerra during 1952-53. He was promoted to brigadier general on January 1, 1970. Until 1970 he was army attaché in Santiago, Chile. In 1970 he was appointed Minister of Fisheries.

Valdez Ángulo, Enrique.

Born on August 16, 1917 in Arequipa. Married to Luz Marina Velasco Guevara, he has two children. He attended the Colegio Nacional de Guadalupe in Lima and entered the Escuela Militar de Chorrillos, graduating in 1940, when he was commissioned a subteniente in the cavalry. He was promoted to brigadier general on January 1, 1968. General Valdez has attended the Armor Officer Basic and Advanced Courses at Fort Knox, Kentucky (1946-47), the Escuela Superior de Guerra (1950-51), the U.S. Army Command and General Staff College, Fort Leavenworth, Kansas (1954-55) and the CAEM (1965). On January 1, 1968 he became commander of the 4th Military Region in Cuzco, and following the military coup that October, became Prefect of Cuzco also. During this time he was appointed President of the Corporación de Reconstrucción y Fomento de Cuzco. On January 1, 1970 he became Director of Intelligence on the Army General Staff. On April 13, 1970, he also was appointed chief of the Sistema de los Complejos Agro-Industriales, in which post he ran the agrarian reform management system. On April 1, 1971 he was appointed Minister of Agriculture.

Vargas Caballero, Luis Ernesto.

Born in Tacna on February 10, 1916. Married to Juanita Cooban Delgado, four children. He graduated from the Escuela Naval and was commissioned ensign on December 30, 1939. He was promoted to rear admiral on January 1, 1968 and vice admiral on January 1, 1972. He attended the Escuela Superior de Guerra Naval in 1952 and the CAEM in 1963. On January 1, 1968 he became chief of the Naval General Staff, serving until his appointment as Minister of Justice on December 13. On April 1, 1969, the Ministry of Justice was abolished, and he became the Minister of Housing, a post he held until his appointment as Minister of the Navy and Commander of the Navy on January 1, 1972. Following a serious dispute with President Velasco in May 1974, he resigned on May 30. The dispute, one of most serious rifts within the Peruvian military establishment since 1968, was created by the opposition of the Navy to the policies of the government relating to the freedom of the press.

Velasco Alvarado, Juan.

Born on June 16, 1910 in Piura. Married to Maria Consuelo Gonzales Posada, with four children. He attended the Liceo San Miguel, and then entered the Noncommissioned Officers School at the Escuela Militar de Chorrillos in April 1929. On December 1, 1929 he was promoted to corporal. Following a nationwide competitive examination, he gained admission as a student at the Escuela Militar, and graduated first in his class in 1934. He was promoted to brigadier general on January 1, 1959 and division general on January 1, 1965. He retired from the Army on January 31, 1969. He attended the Escuela Superior de Guerra (1945-46), and the U.S. Army Caribbean School, Fort Gulick, Canal Zone (1945-46). In January 1959 he was appointed director general of National Marksmanship, serving until April 1960 when he was assigned as commanding general of the 2nd light infantry division in Lima. From February 1962 to January 1964 he was military attaché in Paris, France, when he became an admirer of the policies and style of the late President Charles de Gaulle. During 1964 he was chief of staff of the First Military Region in Piura. From January to June 1965 he was Inspector General of the Army, and then served as a delegate to the Inter American Defense Board in Washington, D.C. From September 1965 to September 1967 he was Chief of the Army General Staff. In September 1967 he became Commander of the Army and acting President of the Joint Command of the Armed Forces. On October 3, 1968 he led the institutional military coup against the government of Fernando Belaúnde Terry and became President of the Revolutionary Government of the Armed Forces.

Villanueva del Campo, Armando.

Secretary General of the Aprista party, he was reelected on July 31, 1974, leading a slate of candidates dedicated to a more defiant policy in opposition to the military government. This was seen as somewhat of a defeat for the policy of conciliation and cooperation favored by the founder of the party, Víctor Raúl Haya de la Torre.

Zileri Gibson, Enrique.

Editor of *Caretas,* one of Peru's leading news magazines. *Caretas* has been closed down by the military government twice for its editorial policies, and Zileri has been deported. The June 1974 closure was for "a completely anti-revolutionary attitude full of insidiousness, falsehoods and insults . . . sowing doubts among the people of Peru about the clear and definite position adopted by the revolutionary government of the armed forces."

Zimmerman Zavala, Augusto.
A professional journalist, he was for many years editor of *El Comercio*. Following the 1968 military coup, he left *El Comercio* to head the Oficina Nacional de Información, and has become the chief spokesman for the official dissemination of information from the Presidential Palace.

Zevallos Gómez, Nicéforo Horacio.
Secretary General of SUTEP, the school teachers union, the antimilitary government union that represents the majority of Peru's school teachers. SUTEP led a successful strike in 1973 which forced the government to arrest the leadership and charge them with opposing the government. In July 1974 all charges were dropped against Zevallos and other leaders in an attempt by the government to bring about a conciliation with the powerful union.

Puerto Rico

Compiled by
Frederick E. Kidder
Director, Graduate School
of Librarianship
University of Puerto Rico

Albors, Juan.
President, Government Development Bank for Puerto Rico.

Alegría, Ricardo E.
Director, Office of Cultural Affairs. Former executive director, Institute of Puerto Rican Culture.

Alonso, José M.
Administrator, State Insurance Fund.

Alonso Alonso, Rafael.
Chairman, Puerto Rico Planning Board.

Álvarez de Choudens, José.
Secretary of Health.

Aponte Martínez, Luis.
Archbishop of San Juan and Cardinal, Roman Catholic Church.

Arrarás Mir, José Enrique.
Secretary of Housing.

Baquero, Jenaro.
President, Housing Bank.

Benítez, Jaime.
Popular Democratic Party (PDP). Resident Commissioner for Puerto Rico in the U.S. House of Representatives; Member, U.S.-P.R. Commis-

sion on the Status of Puerto Rico. Former president of the University of Puerto Rico.

Berríos, Rubén.
Puerto Rico Independence Party (PIP). Senator at Large and Minority Leader for his party; president of the PIP.

Bouret, Roberto.
Executive Director, Company for the Development of Tourism.

Cabranes, José A.
Administrator, Office of Puerto Rico in Washington.

Calero, Astol.
Superintendent, Police of Puerto Rico.

Cancel Ríos, Juan J.
President of the Senate (PDP); Member, U.S.-P.R. Commission on the Status of Puerto Rico.

Casellas, Salvador.
Secretary of the Treasury.

Chardón, Fernando.
Adjutant General, Puerto Rican National Guard. Former Secretary of State.

Colberg, Severo E.
Vice-Speaker of the House of Representatives (PDP).

Cole, Benjamín.
Mayor of Mayagüez (PDP); President of the Association of Mayors of Puerto Rico. Former Postmaster of Mayagüez.

Corrada del Río, Baltazar.
Lawyer and Roman Catholic lay leader. Former chairman, Civil Rights Commission.

Cruz, Ramón A.
Secretary of Public Education.

Cruz de Nigaglioni, Olga.
Representative at Large (PDP); Alternate majority leader.

de Jesús Schuck, Francisco.
Attorney General.

Díaz González, Elisa.
Secretary of Social Services.

Fernández, Ruth.
Singer; Senator at Large (PDP); Chairman, Committee on Arts and Culture.

Ferré, Luis A.
Industrialist, civic leader, philanthropist; Founder, New Progressive Party (NPP). Former governor of Puerto Rico (1969-73).

Folch, Damián.
Secretary of Commerce.

Gallisá, Carlos.
Representative at Large (PIP); vice-president, Puerto Rican Independence Party; minority leader (PIP).

González, Antonio J.
President, Puerto Rican Union Party (PUP); university professor.

González Chapel, Antonio.
Secretary of Agriculture.

Hernández, Dennis W.
Secretary of Transportation and Public Works.

Hernández Agosto, Miguel A.
Vice-President of the Senate (PDP); Chairman, Committee on Socio-Economic Development. Former Secretary of Agriculture.

Hernández Colón, Rafael.
Governor of Puerto Rico, 1973-. Former Attorney General and Senator (PDP).

Hernández Dentan, Federico.
Administrator of Consumer Services.

Marcano, Hipólito.
Senator at Large; Majority Leader (PDP); Masonic and Protestant leader.

Mari Bras, Juan.
Secretary-General, Puerto Rican Pro-Independence Movement.

Mellado Parsons, Ramón.
Senator at Large (NPP). Former Secretary of Public Education.

Méndez, Justo A.
Senator at Large (Independent); member, U.S.-P.R. Commission on the Status of Puerto Rico.

Menéndez Monroig, José.
Senator at Large; Minority Leader (NPP).

Morales, José Ramón.
Representative-at-Large; Majority Leader (PDP).

Morales Carrión, Arturo.
President, University of Puerto Rico. Former Deputy Assistant

Secretary of State for Latin America (Washington, D.C.); former special advisor to the Secretary General of the Organization of American States.

Moscoso, Teodoro.
Administrator of Economic Development.

Muñoz Marín, Luis.
Member, U.S.-P.R. Commission on the Status of Puerto Rico. Founder, Popular Democratic Party; former Senator and Governor of Puerto Rico (1949-64).

Nazario de Ferrer, Sila.
Senator; Alternate Minority Leader (NPP).

Negrón Ramos, Pedro.
Secretary of Natural Resources.

Padilla Ramírez, Hernán.
Representative at Large; Alternate Minority Leader (NPP).

Picó, Rafael.
Economist and geographer. Former chairman of the Planning Board and Secretary of the Treasury.

Pietri Ohms, Rafael.
Chancellor, Mayagüez campus of the University of Puerto Rico.

Pons, Víctor M.
Secretary of State; Member, U.S.-P.R. Commission on the Status of Puerto Rico.

Ramos Yordán, Luis Ernesto.
Speaker of the House of Representatives (PDP); Member, U.S.-P.R. Commission on the Status of Puerto Rico.

Rexach Benítez, Roberto.
Representative at Large (PDP); Chairman, Committee on Natural Resources and Environmental Quality. Former college professor and administrator.

Ríos Sánchez, Ismael.
Executive Director, Corporation for Urban Renewal and Housing.

Rodríguez Aponte, José.
President, Puerto Rico Telephone Company (government owned). Former chairman of the Public Service Commission and executive assistant to the Governor.

Rodríguez Bou, Ismael.
Chancellor, Río Piedras campus of the University of Puerto Rico.

Romero Barceló, Carlos.
Mayor of San Juan; President of the New Progressive Party.

Sánchez Vilella, Roberto.
Engineer. Founder of the People's Party after leaving the Popular Democratic Party. Former Governor of Puerto Rico (1965-69); former Secretary of Public Works and Secretary of State.

Santiago, Basilio.
Controller of Puerto Rico.

Santiago Meléndez, Jaime.
Director, Bureau of the Budget.

Silva Recio, Luis.
Secretary of Labor. Former director of the Graduate School of Public Administration, University of Puerto Rico.

Toledo, José V.
Chief Judge, U.S. District Court for Puerto Rico.

Trías Monge, José.
Chief Justice, Supreme Court of Puerto Rico; Member, U.S.-P.R. Commission on the Status of Puerto Rico.

Viera Martínez, Ángel.
Representative at Large (NPP); Minority Leader (NPP). Former Speaker of the House of Representatives.

Uruguay

Compiled by
Victor C. Dahl
Associate Professor of History
Portland State University

Abdala, Carlos Eduardo.
Minister of Labor, Bordaberry cabinet, June 1972-November 1972. Vice President with President Pacheco, 1967-1971. Blanco party member.

Aguerrondo, Oscar Mario.
Retired army general. Connected with extreme rightwing newspaper, *Azul y Blanco;* considered to be anti-American. Headed Montevideo police force (1963-1967); promoted to general in 1964. Blanco party presidential candidate, 1971. In February, 1973, he participated in the military intervention in civil government.

Alonso, Justo Mario.
Chairman of executive committee of Partido Nacional (Blanco).

Álvarez, Gregorio.
Army general. Head of joint general staff and responsible for the secretariat of the National Security Council (COSENA) during Bordaberry administration. Considered to be a liberal military figure of the *peruanista* group. In July 1972, Tupamaro guerrillas killed his brother, Colonel Artiges Álvarez.

Amestoy, Juan Pedro.
Minister of Commerce, Bordaberry cabinet, April 1972-.

Amorín Larranaga, Julio.
Minister of Labor, first Bordaberry cabinet, March 1972-.

Balparda Blengio, Luis.
Minister of Commerce, November 1972-June 1973. Also served as interim Minister of Education. He was criticized for conducting private business activities while holding public office. Resigned from the cabinet (May 1973) protesting military intervention in civil government. Blanco party member.

Batlle Ibáñez, Jorge.
Congressional deputy. Lawyer, newspaper editor and owner of radio station in Montevideo. Member of Colorado party. Considered to be liberal and pro-Argentine. Son of former President Luis Batlle, whose party leadership position he assumed in 1964 when the father died. His grand-uncle (Jorge) and great-grand-uncle (Lorenz) also were presidents. Colorado presidential candidate in 1966 and 1971. He was instrumental in formulating the constitution of 1966 that ended the collegiate form of government. His congressional supporters, known as *Lista 15 Colorados,* seek to reform the government and the economy. During 1969 Batlle supported President Pacheco; his congressional followers formed a coalition (April 1970) with the Pacheco group to support the administration. A similar agreement with the subsequent Bordaberry administration ended when Batlle was arrested (August 1973) for his opposition activities.

Beltrán, Washington.
Senator. Newspaper executive. As a leader of a conservative Blanco faction, he called for a return to constitutional government after the political crisis of June 1973. Born in 1914. Studied at the University in Montevideo. Served in the chamber of deputies since 1946. National Council of Government; member, 1963-1965; president, 1965-1966.

Blanco Estrade, Juan Carlos.
Minister of Foreign Affairs, Bordaberry administration, November 1972-. Born 1934 in Montevideo, where he attended the university. Until 1965 he worked in the Banco Hipotecario and in the national president's office. Subsequently he has held positions in the Organization of

American States and in the Latin American Association of Free Trade (LAFTA). He directed LAFTA (1968-1971) before serving as undersecretary for foreign affairs (April 1971-November 1972). Blanco has been criticized for alleged connections with the United States government.

Bolentini, Néstor.

Appointed Minister of Interior in Bordaberry cabinet in February 1973, after serving as deputy minister. Member of National Security Council. Although he showed diminishing enthusiasm for the Bordaberry government after suspension of constitutional government in June 1973, he signed the decree of dissolution.

Bordaberry Arocena, Juan María.

President of the Republic; elected November 1971; inaugurated February 1972. Member of Colorado party. Wealthy landowner. A longtime member of the *Movimiento Ruralista* founded in the 1940s. Born in Montevideo (1928) of Basque ancestry; son of Domingo Bordaberry and Elisa Arocena. Attended University of Montevideo. He is married to Josefina Herrán Puig and has seven sons and one daughter. In 1959 he served as chairman of the National Meat Board and later as a member of the Commission for Agricultural Development and the National Wool Board, and chairman of the Committee against Hoof and Mouth Disease. Served in senate, 1962-1964. In 1964 he was the chairman of the Liga Federal de Acción Ruralista, and he served as Minister of Agriculture from 1969 to 1972 in the Pacheco government. Bordaberry had been declared the winner of the contested 1971 election after an army-conducted recount. Opponents contend that his predecessor had designated him to succeed to the presidency. His administration sought to suppress the Tupamaros by military force through invoking legal measures enacted in April 1972. By September 1972, Tupamaro leader Raúl Sendić had been recaptured and 4,000 suspects had been detained. Bordaberry then clashed with the army over its intervention in civil affairs but he acquiesced (February 1973) to the army's insistence on adopting nineteen objectives for regeneration of national politics. These included cleaning up government corruption, agrarian reforms, and army control over security and veto over appointments to the interior and defense ministries. During the June 1973 political crisis, he capitulated to conservatives and suspended the constituion, and in December tried to govern with a council of state formed by cabinet members and supported by the army. His association with the Pacheco regime and continuation of its retaliation policies against leftists and guerrillas weakened his administration.

Bugallo, Marcial.

Second Minister of Labor in Bordaberry government.

Cervetti, Ángelo.

Minister of Works, Bordaberry cabinet, November 1972-.

Charlone, César.

Minister of Economy in various cabinets, 1934-1972. Resigned in April 1971, after being attacked by Frente Amplio. (Died May 8, 1973, aged 76.)

Chiappe Posse, Hugo.

Army general. Commander-in-chief during Bordaberry administration; military chief during Pacheco administration. Known to be a hardliner against the Tupamaros. In February 1973, he forced President Bordaberry to accept the military's nineteen point program for resolving the politico-economic crisis that led to cabinet reorganization.

Cohen, Moisés.

Minister of Economy; member of National Security Council, in Bordaberry cabinet. After the governmental crisis of June 1973, he moved to the budget office. The Blanco opposition attacked him (April 1973) for selling national gold reserves to meet international credit obligations.

Crispo Ayala, Eduardo.

Minister of Public Works, Bordaberry cabinet. Appointed after government crisis of June 1973. Engineer. Conservative civilian.

Echegoyen, Martín Recoredo.

Octogenarian Blanco party politician and leader of conservative congressional group. In April 1970, his group collaborated with the Colorados supporting President Pacheco; in May 1972, the *echegoyenistas* adhered to Bordaberry's government, thereby forestalling an army coup and giving the administration a congressional majority. Echegoyen agreed (December 1973) to serve as head of a council replacing the congress, thus effectively becoming vice president replacing Jorge Sapelli. As a presidential candidate in 1966, he received the second highest number of votes. Served as president of the National Council of Government in 1959.

Echevarría Leunda, Jorge.

Minister of Commerce, first Bordaberry cabinet, March 1972.

Erró, Enrique.

Senator and member of Frente Amplio. In May 1973, the Bordaberry government (especially the military) accused him of sheltering Tupamaros in his home and sought to remove his parliamentary privileges. Erró has been friendly with Peronistas in Argentina, and after the constitutional crisis of June 1973, he formed a resistance committee in Buenos Aires.

Etcheverry Stirling, José.

Minister of Education, Bordaberry cabinet. Appointed after government crisis of June 1973, but he called for a return to constitutional rule. Literature professor. Conservative.

Ferreira Aldunate, Wilson.
Senator. Majority leader of Blanco party in Senate. Unsuccessful presidential candidate, 1971. Ferreira would deal with Tupamaros by fundamental reforms of political, social and economic problems. Opposed rightwing terrorist activities directed against urban guerrillas. Advocated reforms in land systems and banking. Supported by Jorge Batlle's Colorado group. In February 1973, he called for President Bordaberry to resign and later urged impeachment. After the constitutional crisis of June 1973, he formed a resistance committee in Buenos Aires.

Forteza, Francisco.
Minister of Finance, first Bordaberry cabinet, March 1972. Traveled to Europe and the United States in May-June 1972 to negotiate International Monetary Fund loans. Resigned in October 1973, protesting military interference in civil government.

Francese, Antonio.
Retired general. Served as Minister of Defense (February 1973) after charges of scandal had been levelled at his predecessor. Also served as defense minister for Presidents Gestido and Pacheco (1967-1970). While serving as Minister of Interior for Pacheco administration, he took harsh measures (April 1970) against attackers of military installations. Even though he is a strong constitutionalist and enemy of corruption, he resigned from the cabinet (January 1971) protesting what he considered to be weak measures against guerrillas by police and army.

García Capurro, Federico.
Minister of Defense, Bordaberry cabinet, April 1972. Interim Minister of Transport, October 1972. Earlier served as Minister of Education.

Gari, Juan José.
Adviser to President Bordaberry. One of Uruguay's wealthiest men.

Gutiérrez Ruiz, Héctor.
Blanco congressional deputy. While he was president of the Chamber of Deputies, Tupamaro guerrillas captured him (April 1972) and held him for 24 hours while seeking to verify that the Ministry of Interior had supported an illegal death squad to eradicate guerrillas and other opponents. His progressive views have led him to be elected by a Frente Amplio and Blanco coalition as the leader of the opposition to the pro-Bordaberry Colorados in congress.

Iruleguy, Juan Bruno.
Minister of Public Health. Appointed after government crisis of June 1973. Physician. Conservative civilian.

Legnani, Carlos.

Minister of Defense, July-October 1972. First civilian defense minister in thirteen years. Resigned after bad publicity about alleged tortures of prisoners by Bordaberry officials. Representative to United Nations before entering cabinet. Minister of Interior during Gestido administration (March 1967).

Magnani, Enrique.

Army general. Minister of Defense, Bordaberry cabinet, March-July 1972. Considered to be a constitutionalist.

Malet, Armando.

Minister of Defense, November 1972-February 1973. President Bordaberry dismissed him for interferring in civil affairs. Appointed Minister of Economy in April, 1970, and later served as president of Banco Central during Pacheco administration. As a private citizen he sought to negotiate with the armed forces for a return to civilian rule after the June 1973 government crisis.

Medero, Benito.

Minister for Agriculture and Livestock, Bordaberry cabinet, November 1972. Served as interim Minister of Defense in October 1972. Blanco party politician and member of Movimiento Ruralista. As the only Blanco in the cabinet in 1972, he served as Bordaberry's chief supporter in seeking to create a middle-class, multi-party front that would offset Tupamaro influence.

Mora Otero, José A.

Minister of Foreign Affairs, Bordaberry cabinet, April 1972. Replaced (November 1972) by Juan Carlos Blanco Estrade after being attacked in the senate by Frente Amplio. Formerly Secretary General of the Organization of American States.

Murdoch, Omar.

President of Blanco party. Arrested July 1973 and held for six weeks for opposition activities. Retired navy captain.

Narancio, Edmundo.

Minister of Education, Bordaberry cabinet. Appointed after government crisis of June 1973. History professor. Generally regarded as a conservative.

Pazos, Manuel.

Minister of Finance, Bordaberry administration. Appointed July 1973 after constitutional crisis.

Pacheco Areco, Jorge

Newspaper editor and Colorado politician. Ex-president. Born (1920) in Montevideo, son of Manuel Pacheco and Lilina Areco. Educated at the Faculty of Laws and Social Sciences in Montevideo. Edited the Montevideo daily *El Día* until 1965. In 1967 he was elected vice president with the Colorado president, General Oscar Gestido, who inaugurated the presidential system of government under the new constitution of 1966. Pacheco succeeded Gestido, who died in December 1967. Pacheco's administration saw massive inflation, serious labor unrest and the rise of the Tupamaro urban guerrillas, the Movimiento de Liberación Nacional (MLN). A vigorous campaign against the guerrillas failed to suppress them, and other problems defied solution. In the congressional and presidential elections of November 1971, charges of fraud led to an army-supervised recount that awarded the presidency to Juan María Bordaberry, who named his predecessor ambassador to Madrid, March 1972. Pacheco's opponents, many of whom wanted to prosecute him for alleged malfeasance in office, vigorously objected to sending him abroad.

Pereyra Reverbal, Ulises.
Representative for Uruguay, Paraguay and Bolivia to Inter-American Development Bank, Washington, D.C. Longtime political adviser and friend of former President Pacheco. Formerly director of state concern, Usinas y Teléfonos (UTE). Pereyra was kidnapped twice by Tupamaros from 1968 to 1971. In May 1971 he was "sentenced" to life imprisonment in a "people's prison" but a year later was released. Considered to be a spokesman for rightwing elements. In 1973 the military recalled him from Washington to face charges of corruption involving UTE contracts.

Pintos Rizzo, Walter.
Minister of Public Works, Bordaberry administration, March-October 1972. Resigned protesting military interference in civil government.

Presno, Jorge.
Minister of Commerce, Bordaberry administration, 1973. Resigned (July 1973) after government crisis over suspension of constitution.

Purriel, Pablo.
Minister of Public Health, Bordaberry cabinet, November 1972-July 1973. Resigned in protest after suspension of constitution.

Ravenna, Walter.
Minister of Defense, Bordaberry government, February 1973. Also a member of National Security Council. Served as Minister of Interior from November 1972 until entering defense ministry. Signed decree dissolving constitutional government after political crisis of June 1973. Formerly had close connections to President Pacheco.

Robaina Ansó, José María.
Minister of Education, Bordaberry administration. Resigned in protest

against suspension of constitution in June 1973.

Roviro, Alejandro.

Minister of Interior, first Bordaberry cabinet, March 1972.

Sanguinetti, Julio María.

Minister of Education, first Bordaberry cabinet. Resigned October 1972, protesting military interference in civil government. Appointed Minister of Commerce in Pacheco administration, September 1969. A supporter of Jorge Batlle and associated with *desarrollistas* who supported the Pacheco coalition in 1969.

Sapelli, Jorge.

Vice president in Bordaberry administration, 1972-1973. Allegedly selected by President Pacheco to run with Bordaberry to satisfy industrialists. In July 1973 he refused to be a member of the council of state selected by Bordaberry to govern with military backing in place of congress. He was dismissed in December 1973.

Sendić, Raúl.

A founder of Tupamaro urban guerrillas, Movimiento de Liberación Nacional (MLN). Captured in August 1970, and later escaped. Recaptured September 1972; severely wounded in the face. He and thirty others were charged with serious crimes by a military prosecutor. In January 1970 his wife, Violeta Stelich, was arrested after a gunfight. While imprisoned Sendić was permitted to confer with other political detainees. Born in 1926. Formerly a socialist. Studied law, but quit to organize sugar workers in the northern districts. Went underground in 1963 after being linked with theft of arms. In 1964 Argentine police captured him but he jumped bail. Sendić claimed that killing U.S. citizen Dan Mitrione had not been planned by Tupamaros.

Seregni Mosquera, Liber.

Army general. Frente Amplio presidential candidate, 1971. Active opposition to President Bordaberry led to arrest, July 1973; continuing imprisonment made him a popular figure and drew attention to plight of political prisoners. Advocates reform laws for banking, land and industry. During the 1971 campaign two attempts were made to assassinate him.

Servetti, Ángel.

Minister of Public Works, Bordaberry administration, November 1972-. Replaced after government crisis of June 1973.

Trabal, Carlos.

Army general. Chief of military intelligence in Bordaberry administration. He has a reputation for being an intellectual and an opponent of the conservative military faction.

Ubillos, Francisco María.
Minister of Transport, Communications and Tourism, Bordaberry administration.

Urraburu, José Manuel.
Minister of Transport, Communications and Tourism, June 1972-. Subsequently dismissed for permitting opposition speeches.

Vasconsellos, Amílcar.
Veteran Colorado politician and senator. He has filled various ministerial posts in several administrations. An independent and outspoken opponent of the Pacheco and Bordaberry governments' policies of accepting military guidance and direction in civil affairs. In 1973 the military sought to suspend his parliamentary privileges to punish him for making charges that they planned to assume power.

Zerbiño, Ricardo.
Minister of Planning and Budget, Bordaberry government. Member of National Security Council. Resigned July 1973, protesting suspension of constitutional government. He sought to balance the national budget through reduction of civil service and other reforms rather than by increased taxation.

Venezuela

Compiled by
Rand Dee Bowerman
Research Associate,
Center for
Latin American Studies
Arizona State University

Aguilar Mawdsley, Andrés.
Ambassador to the United States, 1974-. Lawyer; received degree from McGill University, Montreal, Canada. Vice-Rector, Universidad Católica Andrés Bello. Minister of Justice 1958-62 and Ambassador to the United Nations 1969-72.

Alvarez Yépez, Froilán.
Agriculture Minister 1974-.

Aristeguieta Schact, Efraín.
Foreign Minister 1974-.

Barrios, Gonzalo.
Chairman of the Acción Democrática (AD) 1968-. Lawyer and political intellectual. Minister of Justice, 1964-68 and AD candidate for President, 1968.

Betancourt, Rómulo.
President of Venezuela, 1958-64. Founder of the AD in 1941. Leader of

the October Revolution of 1945 that sought to establish "progressive reformism." Delegate to the first United Nations Plenary 1946.

Calvani, Arístides.
Professor of Labor Law. Minister of Foreign Relations, 1970-74. Founding member of the Comité por Organización Política y Electoral Independiente (COPEI), the Venezuelan Christian Democratic Party.

Caldera, Rafael.
Lawyer and Professor of Law. A founding member of COPEI and its candidate for President, 1942, 1958, and 1963. Member of the Chamber of Deputies, 1942-44. President, 1959-61. President of Venezuela, 1968-74.

Escobar Salom, Ramón.
Secretary to the President, 1974-.

Fernández, Lorenzo.
Presidential candidate of the COPEI, 1974. Interior Minister, 1970-74; took militant line against Marxist terrorists.

García Bustillos, Gonzalo.
Ambassador to the Organization of American States (OAS), 1974-. Ambassador to the United States, 1964-66.

Hernández Acosta, Valentín.
Minister of Mines and Hydrocarbons, 1974-. Experienced international petroleum engineer. Formulating plans for nationalization of Venezuelan oil fields.

Hurtado, Héctor.
Minister of Finance, 1974-. An economist and expert in monetary planning.

Leal Torres, Homero.
Minister of Defense, 1974-.

Leandro Mora, Reinaldo.
Leader in the AD. Opposed the nomination of Carlos Andrés Pérez in 1974 convention.

Pérez, Carlos Andrés.
President of Venezuela, 1974-. Lawyer; received degree from University at Caracas, 1947. Secretary to the Cabinet, 1960-66. Minister of the Interior, 1966-70. Led reorganization of the AD in 1958.

Pérez de la Cova, Carlos.
Director, Inter-American Development Bank, 1970-. Ambassador to the United Kingdom, 1970-. Received doctorate from the University of Tulsa, 1925. Minister for Economic Affairs, 1961-70.

Pérez-Guerrero, Manuel.

Secretary-General of the United Nations Commission on Trade and Development (UNCTAD), 1969-. Foreign Minister, 1943-44. Finance Minister, 1947-48. Ambassador to the United Nations, 1967-69.

Pérez Jiménez, Marcos.

Dictator of Venezuela, 1952-58. Army Chief of Staff, 1949-52. Convicted and imprisoned four years for the embezzlement of 13.5 million bolívars in public funds. Formed the Cruzada Cívica Nacional (CCN) in 1974 to contest the presidential elections. Expelled by CCN early 1975.

Pinuera Ordaz, Luis.

Director of the AD, 1974-.

Rangel, José Vicente.

Candidate for President in 1974 from the Movimiento al Socialismo (MAS) coalition. Lawyer and socialist, broke with the Unión Democrática Republicana (UDR) in 1964.

Tinoco, Pedro R.

Co-founder of the CCN in 1974. Lawyer; received degree from the Central University at Caracas. Finance Minister, 1969-73. Right-wing deputy in congress; broke with the COPEI in 1973. Founder of the Desarrollista movement.

Villalba, Jovito.

Professor and founder of the UDR in 1946. Unsuccessful Presidential candidate for the UDR in 1963, 1968, and 1974.

132

Center for Latin American Studies Publications

Periodical:
> *Latin American Digest.* Issued quarterly during the academic year.
> Subscription, $2.00 per year. Current volume number is 9.
> *Latin American Digest.* Volumes 1-5 on microfilm. $7.00.

Monograph Series:
> Microfilm, 16mm, negative. Three publications on each reel, $3.00 per
> reel.

Reel 1:
Who's Who in Mexican Government, by Marvin Alisky. 1969.
Latin American Government Leaders, ed. Lewis A. Tambs, *et. al.* 1970.
(For 1975 edition, see CLAS Second Editions.)
Guide to the Government of the Mexican State of Sonora, by Marvin Alisky.
1970.

Reel 2:
Government of the Mexican State of Nuevo León, by Marvin Alisky. 1971.
Bibliography of José Figueres, by Harry Kantor. 1972.*
Peruvian Political Perspective, by Marvin Alisky. 1972. (for 1975 edition,
see last page)

Reference Series:
> *A Look at Publications on Latin American History and Social Sciences,*
> by Elliot Palais. 1973. 30 cents.
> *Directory of Arizona State University Latin Americanists.* 1973. 176 pp.
> $4.50. (out of print)
> *Directory of Arizona State University Latin Americanists.* 1973-74. 200
> pp. $4.50.
> *The Mexican Law of Foreign Real Estate Investment in the Prohibited
> Zones: An Overview, 1971-73,* by Robert S. Tancer and John P. Zanotti.
> 1974. 2nd Edition. $4.25. CIP
> *Latin American Constitutions: Textual Citations,* by Russell H. Fitzgib-
> bon. 1974. $1.50. CIP

Special Studies Series:
> Microfilm, 16 mm, negative. Five studies on each reel, $5.00 per reel.

Reel A:
1 *A Directory of Latin American Political Parties,* by Russell H. Fitzgibbon. 1970.
2 *Mexico in the Organization of American States,* by Lawrence Koslow.
3 *Facilities for Research on Mexico at Latin American Centers,* by
   Lawrence Koslow. 1971.
4 *A Demographic Glance at Argentina's Litoral,* by Paul Hoopes. 1971.
5 *Guatemala's Population Profile,* by Melvin Frost. 1971.*

Reel B:
6 *A Bibliography of Jorge Luis Borges,* by David W. Foster. 1971.*
7 *Barriers to Growth of Local Government in Northern Mexico,* by
   William L. Furlong. 1971.
8 *Bibliography of History and Politics in Brazilian Popular Poetry,* by
   Mark J. Curran. 1972.*

CIP, Library of Congress Cataloging In Publication information

*Also available individually, paper, $1.00.

9 *Chile's Path to Socialism: Observations on Allende's First Year*, by Robert O. Myhr. 1972.*

10 *Economic Impact of Mexican Border Industrialization: A Study of Agua Prieta, Sonora*, by Jerry R. Ladman and Mark O. Poulsen. 1971.

Recent Special Studies, paper only

11 *Military and Paramilitary Forces in Latin America: An Analysis of the Socio-Economic Factors Contributing to Their Dominance*, by Scott McNall. 1973. $1.00.

12 *The Movimiento Nacionalista Revolucionariö: Bolivia's National Party*, by Joseph Holtey. 1973. $1.00.

13 *The Role of Foreign Investments in the Developmental Process: The Case of Mexico, 1884-1911*, by Robert Delorme. 1975. $2.00.

Annual Alberdi-Sarmiento Award Lectures, 1954 to the present: $2.00 each publication. Standing orders accepted.

1 *The Challenge to Pan Americanism*, by Donald M. Dozer. 1972.

2 *Twilight of the Tyrants*, by John S. Knight and Germán Arciniegas. 1973.

3 *Citadels, Ramparts, and Censors: Press Freedom and Dictatorship in Brazil*, by Júlio de Mesquita Filho and Manoel do Nascimento Brito. 1973.

4 *A Future for Latin America*, by Arturo Uslar Pietri. 1974. CIP

5 *Testimonies: Alberdi and Sarmiento in Modern Argentine Life*, by Nicolás Repetto and Victoria Ocampo. 1974 CIP

6 *America at the Crossroads: Parthenon, Yes; Firing Squad, No*, by Efraím Cardozo. 1974. CIP

ALAC-ALAS Proceedings 1973 meeting:

1 *Borges As Concomitant Critic*, by Katharine K. Phillips. *The "Journalistic Page" of the Brazilian Popular Poet*, by Mark J. Curran. 1973. $1.00.

2 *Family Planning in Four Guatemalan Ladino Villages*, by Georgianne Baker. *Credit Union Cooperatives and Development in Guatemala*, by Alfred J. Hagan. 1974. $1.00.

3 *Economic Nationalism in Latin America: An Historical Overview*, by Shoshana B. Tancer. *The Mexican Response to a Favorable World Cotton Market: A Case Study of Mexican Agricultural Development Bank Policy*, by Jerry R. Ladman and Hubert Rieneberg. 1974. $1.00.

4 *The Andean Common Market and Latin American Development*, by Dale B. Furnish. 1974. $1.00.

ALAC-ALAS Proceedings 1974 meeting:

1 *Myth and Reality*, by Esther Crampton. *Novelistic Commentary on Brazilian Sexuality*, by Leo R. Barrow. *The Impact of the Revolution of 1964 on Local Administration in Brazil: The Case of Pôrto Alegre*, by Brent W. Brown. 1974.

2 *Tourism in the Americas: Some Governmental Initiatives*, by Robert Tancer. *Women in the Mexican Labor Force: 1960-1970*, by Breeda C. Dotzler and Jerry R. Ladman. 1975. $1.00.

Hardbound Monographs:

The Spatial Evolution of Greater Buenos Aires, Argentina, 1870-1930, by Charles S. Sargent. 1974 $8.95. CIP Maps charts, illustrations.

Dominican Architecture in 16th Century Oaxaca, by Robert J. Mullen. 1975. $12.95 CIP Illustrations.

Reprint Series:
Soldiers, Indians and Silver, by Phillip W. Powell. 1975. CIP. Paper only, $3.95.
A Voyage to South America, by Antonio de Ulloa, ed. by Irving A. Leonard. 1975. CIP. Paper, $3.75

CLAS Second Editions:
Peruvian Political Perspective, by Marvin Alisky. 1975. Paper, $2.85.
Latin American Government Leaders, ed. by David Foster, 1975. Paper. $3.00

Business Series:
1 *U.S.-Mexico Trade and Investment*
Part 1, *Multinational Firms and Investments in Mexico,* by Hagan, Tancer, Fernández and Mead. 1975. Paper only, $1.50.
Part 2, *El Sistema Financiero Méxicano,* by Albo, Furnish, Maldonado and Garza Botello. 1975. Paper only, $1.50.

Center for Latin American Studies
Arizona State University, Tempe

Director
Lewis A. Tambs

Advisory Council, 1974-75
Georgianne R. Baker
Robert Binninger
Barbara Cox
George Downing
David W. Foster
Dale B. Furnish
J. Douglas Hale
Thomas Karnes
Lawrence E. Koslow
Randi LeGendre
Quino E. Martínez
Robert C. Mings
Katharine K. Phillips
   Recording Secretary
Frances B. Plencner
Susanne Shafer
Jack Shroll

Board of Editors, 1975
Russell H. Fitzgibbon
David W. Foster, Chairman
Jerry R. Ladman
Charles S. Sargent
Noel J. Stowe
Cornelius Zondag